Practical Continuous Testing

make Agile/DevOps real

Zhimin Zhan

Practical Continuous Testing

make Agile/DevOps real

Zhimin Zhan

Contents

Preface

Continuous Testing, simply speaking, is to run all automated functional tests as regression testing multiple times a day, to help software teams deliver high-quality software to production frequently. Continuous Testing (CT in short) was lesser known as Continuous Integration (CI) or Continuous Delivery (CD). Since last year (2019), we hear people talking more about CT, as it is the key process of DevOps.

"Too many jargon words!", some may say. I don't like using jargon words either. Unfortunately, anyone who works in this area needs to understand these terms, because you are going to hear them a lot. In this book, I will use plain English to explain and illustrate techniques, with easy-to-follow hands-on exercises.

The prerequisite of CT is automated functional testing, obviously. If you are new to test automation, please read my other book "Practical Web Test Automation[1]". It puzzled me when I realized some self-proclaimed DevOps/CI specialists had never written a single automated functional test.

My interest in automated functional testing started with HtmlUnit (GUI-less browser testing) in 2005. Shortly after, I discovered Watir, a framework that supports real and visible functional testing in an Internet Explorer browser. Nowadays, I use Selenium WebDriver to test web apps, Appium + WinAppDriver to test Windows Desktop apps and standard Ruby for non-UI functional testing.

Back to my early days on test automation, I was quite happily developing new automated tests and running them individually. Not long after, a big challenge (so obvious but I had never thought of) came: how can I run all test scripts efficiently?

My Continuous Testing journey

My approaches of running all automated tests (as regression testing) have gone through the following stages:

1. **Run tests from IDE**

---

[1]https://leanpub.com/practical-web-test-automation

As a programmer, I naturally tried running functional UI tests in IDEs (including NetBeans and my own TestWise). However, it didn't take long for me to realize that it was wrong. Functional (UI) tests, compared to unit tests, takes much longer to execute. For example, a small suite of 20 tests, each test with an average of 30 seconds execution time, will take 10 minutes. This makes it impractical to run functional tests frequently in IDEs.

2. **Run tests from command line**

To free my IDE (to develop code and tests), I started using build scripts to run tests from the command line. With build scripts, I could also easily add customisation to test executions, such as updating tests from Subversion and excluding certain tests.

A major drawback of running tests from the command line is "No feedback until it completes". Therefore, I turned to a Continuous Integration Server.

3. **Run in CI Server**

In 2006, there was only one CI server available: CruiseControl, developed by Thought-Works. I set up a CruiseControl server to run our Watir test suite. Initially, it worked well. The team could trigger a build easily, view changelog, and build results, all on CruiseControl's web interface. We could act quickly based on feedback.

However, with a growing number of test cases, it was getting harder and harder to pass all tests (a green build). The nature of UI tests, comparing to unit tests, is fragile. A single test step failure, maybe due to an issue on the server or the build machine, failed the whole build. At the same time, the project had become dependent on passing all tests, as the gatekeeper, to release to the production server. Moreover, when a build was failed, developers were not allowed to check in new features, which would complicate the fixing process.

The team embraced automated regression testing, as the benefits were obvious. However, we could not cope with the growing test suites. As a result, the development halted.

4. **Customize CruiseControl with parallel execution, dynamic ordering, ...**

At that time, I could not find an existing solution to reliably run a set of automated UI tests (in Watir) daily. So I decided to extend CruiseControl (thankfully, it was open-source) with features that might improve execution stability and shorten execution time.

The two most important features I had in mind were :

- distributing automated test scripts to multiple build machines to run them in parallel, which greatly reduced the execution time,
- auto-retry of a failed test script on another build machine, to reduce the fragility of overall test execution.

I came up with a design and customized CruiseControl to support parallel testing and auto-retry. The code was by no means of good quality, but it worked. The project was a great success (200,000+ test case executions over 14 months). The team was confident to push the latest green build to production. Looking back, we implemented DevOps more or less in 2009.

5. **Create my own CT server: BuildWise**

CruiseControl was abandoned soon after ThoughtWorks started to work on their commercial CI product, which I did not like. By then, there were a number of CI server products on the market such as Hudson (later renamed to Jenkins) and Bamboo. However, the test executions in those CI servers were suitable for executing unit tests only, and lacked the features for long-running and brittle functional tests. Up to today, I haven't yet seen a single successful Continuous Testing implementation with those CI servers, either non-existing or fake. (My definition of 'Level 1 Success': run 75+ automated UI tests reliably daily).

I decided to create my own Continuous Testing Server with built-in support for the features I added to CruiseControl, and more. Long story short, I started using BuildWise for my own software development in 2012. As of 2020-02-26, the total number of user story level test cases (in Selenium WebDriver) for ClinicWise (one of our web apps) is 608, with over 600,000 test executions over the last 7 years. This enabled us to respond to customers' requests promptly, 95% of customers' feature requests or reported defects were implemented overnight, and available on the production server the next day. By the way, at AgileWay, we never used a defect tracking system (*Note: I am not totally against DFS, just never had the needs in our case, as we are efficient with replicating issues into automated tests and solid regression testing with a good CT process*), and probably never will.

Some of our test automation consulting clients have used BuildWise to replace their failed CI servers. In 2018, BuildWise won the 2nd prize of the prestigious Ruby International Award, judged by Matz, the software legend and the creator of Ruby.

What's unique about this book?

When I studied the "Operating Systems" course at university in 1996, I was deeply impressed by the textbook's author, Prof. Andrew S. Tanenbaum, who actually implemented an operating system: Minix, for teaching purposes. (Prof. Tanenbaum's book and MINIX were Linus Torvalds' inspiration for the Linux kernel [wikipedia[2]]). I gained a lot of insights into CT by designing BuildWise, as well as implementing CT with BuildWise for myself and the clients. I believe that if I do a good job of explaining, readers can benefit from my experiences.

Over the last decade, I have mentored a number of programmers/testers on different projects, and I learned a lot from their perspectives. I built these understandings into BuildWise server as well. For instance, to help new-to-CT professionals to gain confidence, setting up a BuildWise server (from scratch) to run a suite of Selenium tests can be done under 30 minutes.

It is important to note that readers shall focus on the techniques, rather than the actual uses of BuildWise. These techniques are generally applicable, may be implemented in other CT servers, just like what I did to CruiseControl 14 years ago. Treat BuildWise server as a reference implementation, to help you understand the whys and hows, but not limited to it. BuildWise server is free and open-source, you may enhance it or add new features as well.

The example test scripts used in this book are in Selenium WebDriver, the dominant test automation framework for web applications, with RSpec (Ruby binding). Most CT techniques are independent of test automation and syntax frameworks. Three other test syntax frameworks Mocha (JS), PyTest (Python) and Cucumber (Ruby) are covered in Chapter 16.

Who should read this book?

IT professionals who are involved in software development, from testers, programmers, software architects, agile coaches, managers and chief executives, who want to improve the quality of the software and their work life, can benefit from reading this book. It may sound like a bold statement, but it is the feedback I received from some projects whose team members were willing to make a change and embraced the techniques and practices presented in this book. Those projects delivered high-quality software releases frequently, stress-free. You can achieve this too.

---

[2]https://en.wikipedia.org/wiki/Andrew_S._Tanenbaum

People with a basic understanding of the software development cycle will find the texts are easy to follow. Prior experience with automated testing and continuous integration is not necessary. Basic scripting knowledge will help, but again, not necessary.

How to read this book?

I strongly recommend readers to read through chapters in order. More importantly, do the exercises and use new-learned techniques immediately at work. For example, after completing the exercise of setting up BuildWise server to run Selenium tests, try setting up one at work and run a couple of simple real tests for your job. I created video screencasts for most exercises, available on the book site. If you got stuck, watch those videos to see how it is done step by step.

Send me feedback

I would like to hear from you. Comments, suggestions, errors in the book and test/build scripts are all welcome. You can submit your feedback via the book website.

Zhimin Zhan
Brisbane, Australia

1. Introduction

If you are already familiar with the concept of CI/CD and cannot wait to set up your own Continuous Testing (CT) server to run automated functional tests (in a Chrome browser), please feel free to move onto Chapter 2: *setting up a Continuous Testing server* to run a set of Selenium WebDriver tests. After getting it done (in about 30 minutes), come back and read this introductory chapter. It will probably make more sense to you then.

1.1 What is Continuous Testing?

Continuous Testing, according to Wikipedia[1], is *"the process of executing automated tests as part of the software delivery pipeline to obtain immediate feedback on the business risks associated with a software release candidate." The keywords are "**automated tests**", "**delivery pipeline**", "**immediate feedback**" and "**software release candidate**". (*The reason I quote Wikipedia, a non-academic reference, for definitions: because Continuous Testing is new and there are a lot of confusion over it. So I reach for the common understanding at Wikipedia*)

Like many other formal technology definitions, the above sounds right, but not quite clear. Let me interpret:

- **"executing automated tests", "business risks"**

  The automated tests are at the user story level: testing business features. For example, for a web app, the CT process will run a set of automated test scripts to drive the app to verify business functions, in a browser.

  Comparatively, unit testing is conducted by programmers only, that's why unit tests are also called programmer tests.

- **"pipeline", "immediate feedback"**

  In this pipeline, Customers/Business Analysts and programmers are waiting for feedback, and more importantly, ready to act on the feedback. Modification follows feedback, i.e, if there are test failures, a new build (with potential fixes) will be triggered to run another execution of automated tests to ensure the quality.

---

[1] https://en.wikipedia.org/wiki/Continuous_testing

- **"software release candidate"**

  The software is in a ready-to-release state if it has passed all automated functional tests, with little or no human activities on pushing the latest release to production.

Here is my interpretation of Continuous Testing: *"Run automated end-to-end (UI) as regression testing, frequently on new builds. If all tests pass, the software is ready for a production release. If there are test failures, the team must act quickly on the feedback."*

 Continuous Testing is the Holy Grail of Software Development

I didn't invent this term (as much as I would like to take credit for, I heard it from a conversation years ago, but pitifully, could not remember the source), but I think it is a perfect metaphor for Continuous Testing. Yes, it is a big claim, and many of you probably are doubtful. It is my hope to convince you with this book.

Here I share one customer's comments after I helped implement the continuous testing process, which enabled the project to push updates to the production server on a daily basis. This product owner agrees: *"continuous testing is **super valuable** and **super rare**, despite many heard of it, but very few saw it, just like the Holy Grail"*.

1.2 Continuous Testing is the trend

Let's examine some hot IT terminologies (software teams use them every day) over the last two decades.

- 1997 - JUnit by Kent Beck and Erich Gamma

- 1999.07 - "Refactoring" book by Martin Fowler, a process of refining code design backed up comprehensive automated unit testing.

- 1999.10 - First Agile Book by Kent Beck: "Extreme Programming Explained"

- 2000.10 - "Continuous Integration" paper by Martin Fowler

- 2001.02 - "The Agile Manifesto" was written by Kent Beck and other 16 wise software development practitioners

- 2002.11 - "Test Driven Development: By Example" book by Kent Beck

- 2007.07 - "Continuous Integration" book by Paul Duvall, Steve Matyas and Andrew Glover

- 2009.01 - "Agile Testing" book Lisa Crispin and Janet Gregory (Author)

- 2010.08 - "Continuous Delivery" book by Jez Humble and David Farley

- ~2014 - Behaviour Driven Development (BDD)

- ~2018 - DevOps and Continuous Testing (CT)

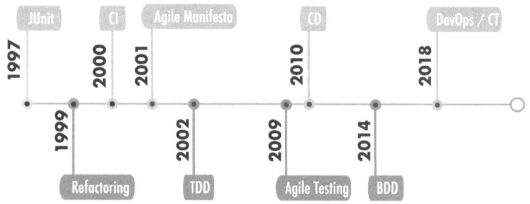

Quite clearly, the trend of software development is moving towards **frequent releases backed up by automated functional testing**.

1. Unit tests ⇒ Functional tests

2. Adhoc test execution ⇒ Repeatable process to run all automated tests

3. Programmers only ⇒ The whole team

4. Testing for better code quality ⇒ Testing for overall quality and frequent releases

This movement shall not come as a surprise, as *being able to push out software releases frequently with high quality* is every software project pursuing. You might have heard of "Quality at speed".

It is worth noting that the practices above (such as unit testing, refactoring, functional testing, and CI/CD) are complementary, rather than replacements. For example, in a software team that embraces a whole-team-involved continuous testing process, programmers are still encouraged to do automated unit testing with TDD.

Can't wait to see running some UI tests in a CT server? you may skip to Chapter 2 (to set up one yourself).

1.3 Continuous Testing vs Continuous Integration

We cannot talk about Continuous Testing without comparing it to "Continuous Integration" (CI in short). Continuous Integration is "*a software development practice where members of a team integrate their work frequently*" [Fowler 00]. In this famous CI article (original version), Martin Flower used "*often talked about but seem to be rarely done*" in the first sentence. Based on my observation over the last two decades, this still remains true: the term CI is favoured by "*talkers*".

CI Reality

I remember at one CITCON (Continuous Integration and Testing Conference) in 2009, a delegate talked about why he attended the conference: "*I want to know how other projects are doing CI? The closest CI experience I ever encountered was that one machine was assigned to do it, then ticked the box. No one touched the machine again.*" Many agreed with him.

A decade later, most software claimed "doing CI" is no more than building (code) and deployment (package), with little or no execution of automated tests …

Demystify CI

"Continuous" in CI means doing integration frequently when the software is ready, NOT "doing it all the time", which is simply impossible and unnecessary. "Integration" in CI means packaging the team's work together (along with dependent third party products) into a release candidate and verify the software works as a whole, the keywords here are '**integrate** and **verify**'. What is the point of integrating a web app 100 times a day but keep showing 'Internal Error' on the home page?

"*Continuous Integration doesn't get rid of bugs, but it does make them dramatically easier to find and remove*" – Martin Fowler

As Martin Fowler pointed out, the main purpose of CI is to help the team to find and fix bugs quicker and easier (via executing automated test scripts), in other words. Automated testing is an essential part of a proper CI process. Now the question comes, why do we rarely see the execution of automated tests in CI?

If we examine the typical CI tasks in a real CI process, it becomes quite clear why incompetent CI specialists exclude the execution of automated tests: **it is hard**.

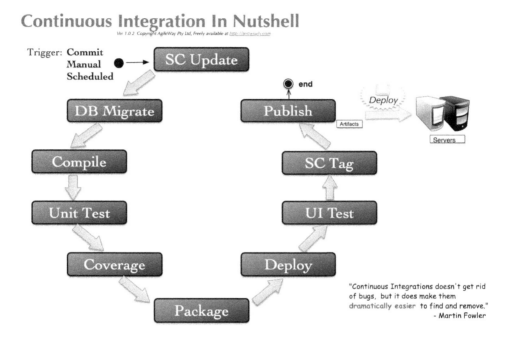

1. **Update source from a version control system** (Difficulty: *easy*)

   This is a built-in CI feature, and you don't usually need to do anything for this step, except installing the source control command line (or called client) tools.

2. **Database Migration** (Difficulty: *medium* or *hard*)

   During the life of software development, inevitably, your database schema needs changes along with the development, and in fact, quite frequently. For example, creating a new table or adding a new table column. This needs to be done systematically.

3. **Compile** (Difficulty: *easy*)

This only applies to compiled languages such as Java or C#, You don't need this step if using a dynamic language such as Ruby.

4. **Unit Testing** (Difficulty: *hard*)

   Unit test, as the key concept of Test Driven Development, helps programmers to produce not only robust code, more importantly, but also better-designed code. If a piece of code is hard to write the unit test for it, its design is most likely not optimal.

   Programmers who claim 'refactoring code' without a suite of unit tests really are 'cowboys change with hope for good luck'. No unit tests, no code refactoring.

5. **Code Coverage** (Difficulty: *medium*)

   Code coverage is measuring the percentage of code (in terms of methods/lines) that is covered by unit tests. This helps to find out untested and redundant code, to keep source code tidy and lean. It is also a good incentive for Test-Driven Development.

   In reality, achieving 100% code coverage is often not practical, 80% is already a good figure. As a matter of fact, you may find many projects without code coverage data or at a single-digit percentage.

   By including code coverage into the build process, we can help new/junior (not by age) programmers to develop the habit of writing unit tests.

6. **Package** (Difficulty: *medium*)

   A software release package typically contains compiled source code, configurations, web pages (with CSS and JavaScript), file templates, ..., etc. This step is mostly concerned with how to package files using build scripts into a specific format. For example, a war file is a zipped file format used for web applications developed in Java.

7. **Deploy** (Difficulty: *easy* or *medium*)

   Depending on the nature of your application, deployment can be quite complex (if heavyweight frameworks are used) or very simple (such as Ruby on Rails). A typical deployment process consists of the following steps:

   1. Stop the server if it is currently running

   2. Unpack the new release

   3. Update the database schema (database migration).

   4. Update configuration

   5. Start the server

Deployment needs to be simple, reliable, and quick. With the popularity of cloud deployment, new deployment technology emerges such as Chef, Docker/Kubernetes containers. Unfortunately, many DevOps engineers (by the way, I think it is a wrong title for a person who solely does deployment, as deployment is only counted for about 5% of DevOps work from my experiences) don't use them well. More often than not, they make deployment over-complicated, and as a result, fragile and slow.

In 2019, all projects I witnessed using Docker/Kubernetes containers were not good. One was particularly bad, I have never seen a deployment process that was so fragile (and slow) in my over 20 years of IT career (even worse than the dark days using EJB containers). The test servers (a batch of containers) can barely function properly for one day. But I did learn one thing new: "run out of inodes" error (I learned from the Operating System course at Uni) can actually happen.

I am not against new deployment technologies, given they can indeed increase productivity and simplify the work. If the end results are completely opposite to your goal, stop and revert it back until you find the right person who can actually do it properly. There are plenty of costly lessons in the software industry of blindly following new hypes.

WhenWise deployment in 12 seconds

The below is a typical deployment log of WhenWise, one of my web applications written in Ruby on Rails. The deployment tool is **mina**[a], basically an old-school executing a series of batch scripts via SSH.

```
$ mina production deploy
-----> Fetching new git commits
-----> Using git branch 'master'
       Cloning into '.'...
       done.
-----> Using this git commit
       Zhimin Zhan (06405f79):
       > bump ver 0.8.30
-----> Symlinking shared paths
-----> Installing gem dependencies using Bundler
-----> DB migrations unchanged; skipping DB migration
-----> Skipping asset precompilation
-----> Cleaning up old releases (keeping 5)
       /var/www/rails/whenwise/tmp/build-157846690712699
-----> Deploy finished
-----> Building
```

```
-----> Moving build to /var/www/rails/whenwise/releases/561
-----> Build finished
-----> Launching
-----> Updating the /var/www/rails/whenwise/current symlink
       /var/www/rails/whenwise/current
-----> Loading rbenv
-----> Quiet sidekiq (stop accepting new work)
       /var/www/rails/whenwise/current
-----> Stop sidekiq
       Sidekiq shut down gracefully.
-----> Start sidekiq
-----> Update crontab for ap11.agileway.net_au
       [write] crontab file updated
-----> Done. Deployed version 561
       Connection to whenwise.com closed.
       Elapsed time: 12.24 seconds
```

The deployment script (under 160 lines) performs the following tasks:

1. Get new code (`git pull`),

2. Update/install dependent libraries, not necessary in this case.

3. Database migration, no need for this deployment as

4. Precompile JS/CSS assets, no need for this deployment.

5. Package for release

6. Stop queue process (Sidekiq)

7. Start the queue process

8. Verify/Update cron job

9. Reload the app

If there are database changes or new libraries to be installed, the scripts will apply installations as necessary.

For my every CI build, our deployment steps will deploy the updates to 9 test servers: ci1.whenwise, ci2.whenwise, ..., ci9.whenwise. Then automated tests will be run against these test servers. We will cover the set-up in later chapters. Here, I just want to emphasise the importance of quick and reliable deployment, which is the prerequisite task of CT.

---

[1]https://github.com/mina-deploy/mina

8. **Functional Testing** (Difficulty: *very hard*)

   Executing automated functional tests against the test server(s) with a new version of software deployed (by the last step), essentially, Continuous Testing.

   Some might not agree with the difficulty (**very hard**) I rated there.

   I would say we might have different perspectives. Most UI testing, if present, in CI is no more than smoke and mirrors. For me, CT is the core of software development. If all automated functional tests pass in CI, this build will be released to production. (For nearly all user stories and customer-found defects, I have automated tests for them).

   Let me illustrate it by an example. Let's say that we have 200 user-story-level functional tests written in Selenium WebDriver, on average, one test case has 30 test steps (each step represents a user operation, such as entering text, clicking a link and verifying certain text) and execution time of a single test is 30 seconds. In total, there are 30 x 200 = 6000 test steps and a full regression testing will take 6000 seconds. To get a green build (all tests pass), each of every 6000 test steps needs to pass within nearly 2 hours of test execution. A single failure results in a broken build.

   Now, do you agree this is a very, very hard task?

9. **Tag a build/release** (Difficulty: *easy*)

   Tagging refers to labelling the repository at a certain point of time so that it can be easily retrieved in the future to achieve repeatable builds.

   You don't have to label every build, probably only for the green builds (which have passed all tests). Be aware of the time difference between checking out from source control and actual tagging. A common approach is to introduce 'Code Freeze' or schedule full builds at night time.

10. **Publish** (Difficulty: *easy*)

    Once a build finishes, besides showing build status and other information on CI's web interface, there are numerous ways to publish the result, such as email, Slack, or even switching on a lava lamp.

Apart from the success/failure indicator, build results might also highlight failed test cases and artifacts (files generated out of the build process). Most CI servers keep the build history, which can be generated into pretty charts for reporting purposes.

As you can see, there are three hard tasks (in the order of difficulty): "**Database Migration**", "**Unit Testing**" and "**Functional Testing**". Few will deny the needs of these steps, though most probably have never seen them done properly.

This book is to help you to implement CT, the most challenging and rewarding task in CI: execution automated functional tests.

Tips for Database Migration and Unit Testing Tasks

This is a CT book, so I will be light on these.

- **Database Migration**
  Study the database migration approach in Ruby on Rails[a], you might be able to work out a feasible approach. For one Java project, I embedded Ruby on Rails's database migration scheme directly in the project code, then use JRuby to invoke database migration in CI.

- **Unit Testing**
  There are plenty of books and online resources on this topic. However, in practice, despite the majority of programmers acknowledging the benefits of unit testing, unit testing is mostly done adhocly. The fundamental reason, I think, is that programmers lack knowledge of good unit testing practices. Please read 'A Set of Unit Testing Rules'[b] by Michael Feathers.

[a]https://edgeguides.rubyonrails.org/active_record_migrations.html
[b]https://www.artima.com/weblogs/viewpost.jsp?thread=126923

If CI is implemented properly, no need for CD or CT

CI has been so messed up in practice that it is becoming meaningless. That is why a new term comes up "Continuous Delivery" (CD in short, which later quickly lost its meaning as well), somehow people find it fancier to say these two terms together "CI/CD". In every project I visited over the last decade, agile coaches/architects talked a lot about CI/CD and did not do hands-on test automation, their continuous integration processes were all embarrassing failures.

Once I worked at a software company, they had a Bamboo CI server with a number of projects, which seldom ran and virtually no sign of executing automated tests. However, they claimed they were providing CI consultancy to one of the top four banks in Australia.

If CI's main purpose is to build a releasable software package, this has been achieved years ago with build scripts, like an Ant task generating a deployable war file (back to J2EE days). Triggering a build from a web interface and seeing build results (on CI server) is nice, but don't you think there is not much to brag about? The purpose of CI is to ensure quality releases by running automated tests against release candidates. The testing is the main part.

Some people might say "Continuous Testing" could be the next ruined 'talker term'. Yes, that could well be true, and probably already is. At this moment, we have run out of terms, sadly. I will settle with the term "CT", because of its emphasis on testing.

So what is the relationship between CT and CI? In simple words, CT is a part of CI, the most important and difficult part. If a CI process is implemented well, there is no need for "CD" or "CT".

 "Continuous Delivery is really about testing"

The origin of 'Continuous Delivery' is the book with the same title by Jez Humble and David Farley, published in 2009. Some will debate the differences among CI, CD and CT. Frankly, I don't think it is necessary. The core of all three is the same: executing automated functional tests as regression testing.

Don't just take my word for it, let's hear the views from the authors of the Continuous Delivery book and a highly claimed authority in this field. In an interview[2] in October 2019, Lisa Crispin, the co-author of Agile Testing book, said this: "They (Jez Humble and David Farley) asked me to be a technical reviewer for their manuscript (Continuous Delivery book) … I read it. It's a book about testing, you know, the whole book is really about testing. That's the heart of continuous delivery. Jez Humble is very supportive of my saying that."

1.4 Separate CT from existing CI/CD

If CI is real, it would run automated functional tests as a part of build tasks, However, this is a big 'if'. For software teams who are about to embark on the journey of CT, I recommend separating from your existing CI process, as your current CI/DevOps engineers most likely had no knowledge or experience of running automated functional tests in CI.

By separating the CT process out, you may avoid

- be forced to use a particular CI product.

  The techniques and hardware requirements (as you will see in later chapters) are quite different from executing unit tests. By following the existing CI process (with a

---

[2](https://www.infoq.com/articles/current-future-testing/)

particular server product), without a doubt, the perspective has been set in unit testing, which is wrong.

I have never seen a single successfully implemented CT using Jenkins, Bamboo, TeamCity, GitLab, ..., etc, these so-called popular CI servers. This does not mean CT is impossible with them. Back in 2006, I implemented most of the techniques in this book as a Java plugin to CruiseControl (the first CI server), with a good outcome. So technically, it is possible with all CI servers. However, this requires quite a lot of work.

- be forced to use a certain test script syntax and framework.

  Different from unit testing, the functional test script syntax can be in a different programming language. For example, I have implemented CT with functional test scripts in Ruby for products developed in Java, C#, JavaScript, and Ruby.

- be asked to follow certain inappropriate practices

  This may include version control policies (a bad example: branching on each user story), directory structures, naming conventions, ..., etc.

1.5 Continuous Testing vs DevOps

"By 2020, DevOps initiatives will cause 50% of enterprises to implement continuous testing using frameworks and open-source tools." – Predicts 2017: Gartner Report[3]

If I ask you the hottest term in the software development industry in the past 2 years, many will say "DevOps". Frankly, I think the term DevOps is quite vague (opposed to '10-minute build' and 'pair programming'), therefore, is open to interpretation.

I have heard a few DevOps talks, however, they left no marks on my brain. For one project I witnessed in 2019, the executives got sold by the 'impressive talk' by a 'DevOps talking-expert', engaged the consulting company to implement DevOps. These consultants were busy talking, presenting, introducing new software ..., for a few months. The result was a total disaster, in the end, the teams were told to revert back to the old way. The reason is simple: the foundation of DevOps is Continuous Testing. It is easy to understand, just imagine a pipeline producing poor quality products in a factory. As we know, the quality problems magnify in an order of magnitude.

---

[3]https://www.gartner.com/doc/3525622/predicts--application-development

Continuous Testing ➝ DevOps
~~**Continuous Testing**~~ ➝ Dev Oops

Let's switch the focus to DevOps' objective (instead of its definition). I resolve to Wikipedia[4]: "*It (DevOps) aims at establishing a culture and environment where building, testing, and releasing software can happen rapidly, frequently, and more reliably*". This sounds quite like the objective of Continuous Integration, doesn't it? Except with an emphasized focus on quality releases and feedback to the team. For example, if you set up a Jenkins or TeamCity project to build software and run a few unit tests (i.e. programmer tests), you might call it CI, but it is incomplete in terms of DevOps, as it does not include regression testing (at the functional level) for releases.

I don't mind DevOps at all. As a matter of fact, I have been developing software this way (releasing high-quality software frequently with comprehensive automated testing) since 2007, and have shared my experience in numerous presentations. Only at that time, the term "DevOps" and "CT" did not exist yet.

1.6 Reality Check

Despite all the hype of CT (and previously CI/CD) and DevOps, the reality is 99%+ software teams at level 0 (*a term I borrowed from the movie: Kungfu Panda*) on CT. If you are not convinced, try to answer the two questions below:

- When was the last time your project pushed a release to the production?

- How often do you do that?

In the context of DevOps, the correct answers for the above are "Yesterday" and "At least once a day".

I have my reasons for using 99%+. Alan Page, the first author of "How We Test Software at Microsoft" book, said this at Test Talk PodCast #44, March 2015[5] "*95% of the time, 95% of test engineers will write bad GUI automation just because it's a very difficult thing to do correctly*". Alan's view remains unchanged since 2008, when he wrote on his blog[6] "*For 95%*

---

[4]https://en.wikipedia.org/wiki/DevOps
[5]https://testguild.com/podcast/automation/44-alan-page-testing-software-at-microsoft-lessons-learned/
[6]https://angryweasel.com/blog/gui-schmooey/

of all software applications, automating the GUI is a waste of time. For the record, I typed 99% above first, then chickened out. I may change my mind again."

Alan used '99%' there, I added '+' because most software companies won't match Microsoft on

- quality of software test engineers

- resources (both technically and financially)

Furthermore, Continuous Testing adds more challenges, by running the whole test suite as regression testing frequently.

1.7 Why will this book help?

I know some might think: *"if CT is almost mission impossible, how could I believe that you can do it?"*. I understand no matter what I say, it probably won't be enough to convince you. Instead, I write this book (and produced videos on the book site) to guide you in implementing CT step by step.

In the next chapter, I will show you how to set up a CT server and run a set of Selenium WebDriver tests, under 30 minutes.

2. Set up a CT server to run Selenium tests in minutes

While Continuous Testing (CT in short) is not a new term, it remains mysterious to many people, as they have never seen it working in software projects. In this chapter, I will show you how to set up a continuous testing server to run a set of Selenium WebDriver tests, on your machine, in a matter of minutes.

2.1 Objectives

- Install and set up a CT server (BuildWise)

- Create a CT project for a set of existing test scripts

- Trigger a test execution of all test scripts with a click of a button

- See test execution results on CT Server

Estimated time: 10 - 30 minutes. The majority of the time will be spent on installing prerequisite software such as Ruby and its libraries. If you have already had them on your machine, it will be much quicker.

Setting up a continuous integration/testing server from scratch might sound intimidating for some. Don't worry, I am quite confident you can get it done after following the instructions in this chapter. Also, you can find step-by-step screencast videos on the book site.

The environment for this exercise is Windows platform. For macOS/Linux users, the same steps can be done in a very similar process.

You don't need to worry about the test script syntax yet, it is RSpec by the way. I will cover test syntaxes in later chapters. For now, just focus on our main objective here: run a suite of functional tests (in this case: Selenium WebDriver tests for a web application) in a CT server.

2.2 Prerequisite

1. **Install Git**

   Git is now the industry standard version control system for software development. Most likely, Git is already installed on your machine.

   To verify Git installation, run `git --version` in a command window. You shall see the output like below.

   ```
   git version 2.18.0.windows.1
   ```

   If you haven't got Git, get it from the Git site[1]. The installation is very easy.

2. **Install Ruby**

   BuildWise CT server requires Ruby (a popular scripting language) to run it.

   - macOS

     Ruby is already included in macOS. You may use *rbenv* or *rvm* to install a specific Ruby version.

   - Linux

     Use standard package tool to install, usually just one command such as `sudo apt install ruby-full` on Ubuntu.

   - Windows

     Download RubyInstaller for Windows[2] with Devkit, such as '*Ruby+Devkit 2.6.4-1 (x64)*'. The DevKit is required for compiling certain libraries (called Gem in Ruby).

     Run the installer. After it completes (don't forget the DevKit setup part), run the command below in a new command window.

     ```
     > gem install bundler --no-document
     ```

     > If you encounter some issues on starting up the server (Windows only), try run the commands below:
     >
     > ```
     > > gem install sqlite3 --platform=ruby
     > > gem install ffi --platform=ruby
     > ```

---

[1] https://git-scm.com/
[2] https://rubyinstaller.org/

> These two libraries need to be compiled (using DevKit) to work on your machine.

3. **Browser drivers** (such as ChromeDriver for Chrome)

To run Selenium WebDriver tests against Chrome browser, besides the Chrome browser itself, you need to install ChromeDriver[3].

- go to ChromeDriver site[4]
- Download the one for your target platform, unzip it and put **chromedriver** executable in your PATH.

Download the correct version to match your Chrome browser and drop it (*chromedriver.exe* on Windows) into a folder in your PATH, for example, `C:\Ruby26-x64\bin`.

To verify the installation, open a command window (terminal for Unix/Mac), execute command `chromedriver --version`, You shall see texts like below:

```
ChromeDriver 89.0.4389.23
```

To run tests in a different type of browser, install its matching driver, such as GeckoDriver for Firefox. Selenium site[5] has the details for all browser types.

2.3 Install CT Server

The Continuous Testing server we are going to use is BuildWise, a free and open-source CT server created by me (*BuildWise won the 2nd prize of the Ruby Award in 2018*). You may use it for the job, your clients, and own projects.

Please note that the techniques I presented in this book are generally applicable to other CT servers. In fact, some features I firstly implemented for CruiseControl (the grand-daddy of CI servers), as a plugin, back in 2007.

---

[3]https://chromedriver.chromium.org/downloads
[4]https://sites.google.com/a/chromium.org/chromedriver/downloads
[5]https://selenium.dev/downloads

1. **Download BuildWise Server**

   Download BuildWise server (in zip format, e.g. buildwise-1.8.9.zip) from TestWisely[6], unzip to a folder. For example, *c:\agileway\buildwise-1.8.9.*

   Open a command window (or terminal on macOS/Linux).

   ```
   cd buildwise-1.8.x
   ```

   Run the `gem-install.bat` *(macOS/Linux users:* `gem-install.sh`*).*

2. **Start up BuildWise Server**

   Run `startup-demo.bat` (or `start-demo.sh` on macOS/Linux) under the folder to start the BuildWise server. If you see the text below, the server is started successfully.

   ```
   * Listening on tcp://0.0.0.0:3618
   Use Ctrl-C to stop
   ```

   Open *http://localhost:3618* in your browser.

   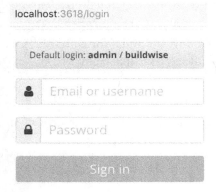

3. **Login**

   The default login/password: *admin/buildwise.*

---

[6]http://testwisely.com/buildwise/downloads

2.4 Create a Build Project

BuildWise uses the concept of 'Project' to confine the settings and build activities on how you execute tests. A quick way to create a project in BuildWise is to provide a name (for displaying), an identifier, and a local working folder that contains test scripts. To make it easy for beginners, BuildWise includes a set of sample project configurations (with code hosted on Github) for different test frameworks.

1. Prepare a sample test project

   I created some sample Selenium WebDriver projects on Github[7]. Clone it to your machine using Git.

   ```
   cd c:\work
   git clone https://github.com/testwisely/agiletravel-ui-tests.git
   ```

   You will get a set of Selenium test projects under *c:\work\agiletravel-ui-tests*. Run the commands below to install the libraries to run the test scripts in this project.

   ```
   c:\work\agiletravel-ui-tests\selenium-webdriver-rspec
   install-lib.cmd
   ```

   Run a sample test script to verify.

   ```
   rspec spec\01_login_spec.rb
   ```

   You shall see test execution in a new Chrome browser window. The output will be like the below:

   ```
   ..

   Finished in 9.37 seconds (files took 0.4117 seconds to load)
   2 examples, 0 failures
   ```

2. Click "**New Project**" on BuildWise

3. Click the "**Fill demo project**" dropdown (on the top right) and select "**RSpec**". BuildWise will populate settings for a demo project.

---

[7]https://github.com/testwisely/agiletravel-ui-tests.git

4. Change "**Working Folder**" to the location of your prepared test project, *c:/work/agiletravel-ui-tests*

5. Click the "**Create**" button

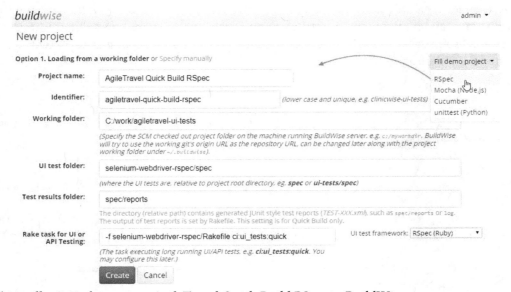

This will create the project *AgileTravel Quick Build RSpec* in BuildWise.

2.5 Trigger test execution manually

To start a build (for our purpose, 'Build' means the execution of a suite of automated functional tests), click the '**Build Now**' button.

The colour of the lava lamp image (of the project) is now changed to orange, indicating a build is underway.

Soon you will see a browser window launched, and your test is executed in it.

2.6 Feedback while test execution in progress

If the build page is not shown already, click a build label (such as '1:building') to show details of test execution:

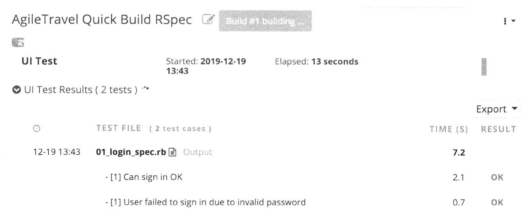

You can see the results of a test script as soon as it finishes the execution, no need to wait for the whole suite to complete. The above screenshot was taken when the first test script (containing 2 test cases) finished execution.

If there are test failures or errors, they will be displayed on BuildWise's web interface.

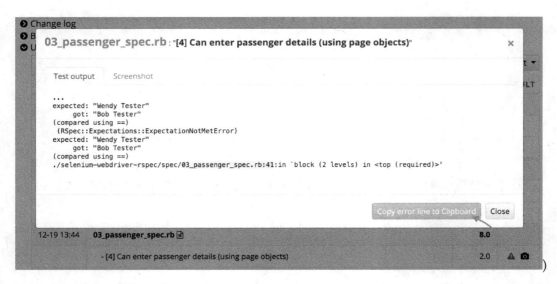

From the error or failure description, experienced test engineers have a good chance to guess the cause right. If not, we can navigate to the test case where the error occurred, with the highlighted test file name and line number.

Please note that the tests are executed on the build server, not on your machine (unless you are running the BuildWise server locally). You may open the test project in TestWise on your computer and run a test-of-interest, and don't have to wait for the CI build to complete.

2.7 Build finished

When a test execution completes, you will get the full test results shown on BuildWise. In the build below, one out of six automated test cases failed.

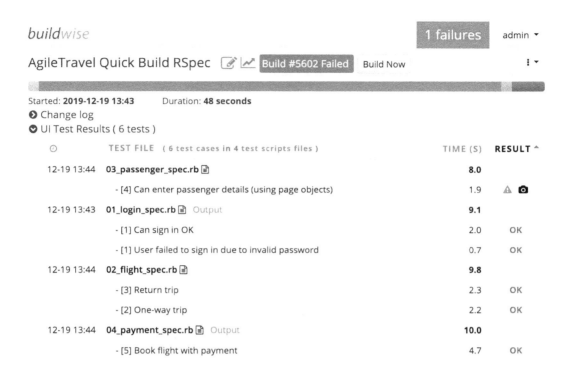

Visit the home page of the BuildWise server, a red lava lamp image is shown next to the project.

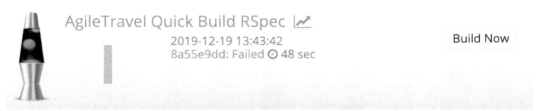

A red lamp! You might naturally think: how do I fix the build? In Chapter 3, we will do an exercise to fix this broken build. For now, just assume it will be fixed by the next user commit. Trigger another build on the CT server. The commit message and changed files are shown on the new build.

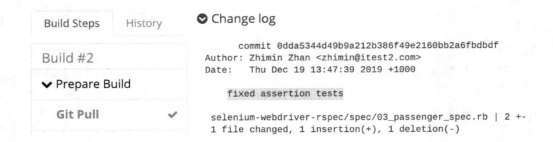

If all tests pass, you will be rewarded with a green lava lamp on the dashboard page.

2.8 Common Errors

1. Build task not found

   Error in log: (*Expand "Build log" to view*)

   ```
   2019-12-17 13:12:12 +1000 [ERROR] {Builder} run task error |
   dir : /Users/zhimin/.buildwise/work/agiletravel-quick-build-rspec/sources
   command : rake -f selenium-webdriver-rspec/Rakefile ci:ui_tests:not_exists .. 2>&1
   exitstatus: 1
   ```

   Fix: verify the task by running the command: `rake ...` from a command window.

2. ChromeDriver not installed

   ```
   Unable to find chromedriver. Please download the server from
   https://chromedriver.storage.googleapis.com/index.html and place it somewhere on your
   PATH. More info at https://github.com/SeleniumHQ/selenium/wiki/ChromeDriver.
   ```

   Fix: Download chromedriver and put it under a folder in PATH.

3. ChromeDriver version does not match Chrome browser's

```
session not created: This version of ChromeDriver only supports Chrome version 87
(Selenium::WebDriver::Error::SessionNotCreatedError)
```

Fix: Upgrade (or downgrade) your chromedriver version.

4. Bundler version issue

If you see an error such as '*This Gemfile requires a different version of Bundler*' or '*You must use Bundler 2 or greater with this lockfile.*' on running gem-install.bat, it means that the version of Bundler (that comes with Ruby) needs to be updated.

```
> gem install bundler --no-document
```

Then rerun gem-install.bat.

5. Required libraries not installed.

```
Gem::MissingSpecError:
  Could not find 'selenium-webdriver' (>= 0) among 116 total gem(s)
  Checked in 'GEM_PATH=C:/Ruby26-x64/lib/ruby/gems/2.6.0'
# ./selenium-webdriver-rspec/test_helper.rb:2:in `<top (required)>'
```

or

```
LoadError: cannot load such file -- httpclient
```

Fix: install the missing library from command line.

```
> gem install selenium-webdriver
> gem install httpclient
```

6. Ruby DevKit (windows only) not installed

Some invalid values for certain environment variables such as RUBYOPT could be the reason. Run gem list command might reveal the issue. If that's the case, remove those environment variables.

Fix: run ridk install from the command line.

3. How Continuous Testing Works?

In the previous chapter, we did a quick set up to run Selenium WebDriver tests in a BuildWise server. In this chapter, we will dive deeper to see the core components and steps in CT. Along the way, I will show the steps to install BuildWise server that fits for production use.

3.1 Terminology

First of all, let me clarify some terminologies used in BuildWise server.

1. **Server**

   BuildWise server runs on a port number (default to 3618) and provides a web interface.

   Change to port 80 if you can

   Port 80 is the default port for HTTP, it is better to use port 80 if you can, for two reasons:

   - It is unlikely to be blocked for users (and build agents, more on this in later chapters)
   - The server URL is shorter (without the port number)

   To change the port, edit the *startup-demo.bat* file.
   ```
   rackup -p 3618
   ```

2. **Project**

   A BuildWise project defines how we run tests against a software build. Here are some sample CT projects:
   - Quick run a handful of key tests for Software A
   - Full regression testing of all automated tests for Software A
   - Generation test data for Business Analysts for Software B
   - Full regression testings for Software A on UAT (User Acceptance Testing) environment

3. **Build Server Working directory**

The directory where BuidWise stores its settings and checked-out test scripts. It is set to use *BUILDWISE_HOME* environment variable. On Windows, you can change it in *startup-demo.bat*.

```
set BUILDWISE_HOME=C:\agileway\.buildwise
```

4. **Build**

We often see a build number next to a software version, e.g. v2.0.5 build 1030, where 1030 is the build number. The build number is incremental, and is usually set in the packaging step of the CI process. There might be a Build #1029 for version 2.0.5, but it didn't make to the release status due to not passing the quality check.

A '*Build*' in BuildWise server simply means performing a series of build tasks such as executing automated tests on a software build candidate. If all tests pass, this build is considered to be a valid release candidate. Software teams may use the BuildWise build number to identify a release.

5. **Build trigger**

A Build may be triggered in three ways:
- Manually - via UI

  User starts a build via the server's web interface, like what we just did.

- Scheduled - via API

  A build is scheduled (via CT server's API) to run at a certain time, e.g. 12:00 PM for doing builds when the team is on lunch breaks.

- Repository hooks

  A build is triggered on operations on the version control system (e.g. Git). For example, setting up a Git commit hook to invoke CT server's API to start a build.

6. **Build Task**

CT server, simply speaking, provides a web interface to executing a series of tasks with ease. A build task, technically speaking, runs a command (commonly in a form of build scripts). If the return code of the command is 0, the task is considered 'successful', then the CT process moves onto the next build task, until the end. If the return code is NOT 0, the task was 'failed', and the whole CI build ends with a 'failure' status.

We will examine the build task in detail later.

3.2 CT Process in detail

After a typical CT process is started (by manually triggered or scheduled), it performs the following tasks:

1. **Check out from Git repository**

   This task is performed automatically by BuildWise server. We always want to run the latest test scripts. This task does standard `git pull` to get them from the parent Git repository.

2. **Prepare**

   Run user-specified scripts to get the test environment ready for executing automated tests.

3. **Execute Automated Functional Tests**

   The core task of CT, obviously, is to run all or a suite of automated tests.

4. **Show Test Results**

   Display the test results (out of the JUnit XML report generated from the text executions) on CT server's web interface.

5. **Notify**

   Besides the final test report on CI's web interface, CI may send build notifications in other forms, such as Email, Slack and Smart Power Plugs (to turn on/off power).

3.3 Install BuildWise Server for production use

 Continuous Testing requires broad knowledge, such as database, operating systems, scripting, network, ..., etc. A good Continuous Testing engineer needs to be open-minded and embrace continuous learning.

In Chapter 2, we started the BuildWise server with the command *start-demo.bat* (or *start-demo.sh* on macOS/Linux), which suggests it is for demonstration purposes. But what about production use? The good news is that the actual BuildWise server setup is already complete, just need to set up a proper SQL database.

A BuildWise server in demo mode runs on a single-file-based SQLite3 database, which is not optimal for production use. For production use, we suggest using MySQL (or a variant such as MariaDB), "the world's most popular open-source database[1]".

Firstly, here is a database configuration of the BuildWise server, in **config/database.yml** file:

```
demo:
  adapter: sqlite3
  database: db/buildwise_demo.db
  timeout: 15000

production:
  adapter: mysql2
  encoding: utf8
  database: buildwise_production
  host: 127.0.0.1
  pool: 10
  username: root
  password: buildwise
```

1. Install MySQL Community Server

   Download and install the free MySQL Community Server. Make sure you note down the password you set for the **root** user.

    During MySQL setup, select 'Use Legacy Authentication Method'.

2. Verify mysql2 gem

   mysql2 is the standard Ruby library to work with a MySQL database. Run gem `list mysql2` to verify whether it is installed on your server machine. If not, run gem `install mysql2` to install it.

3. Create BuildWise Database

   Create a new MySQL database for BuildWise server:
   `mysqladmin -uroot -p create buildwise_production`

4. Edit **config/database.yml** to set the password

   Change the password under `production:` section.

---

[1]https://www.mysql.com/products/community/

5. Start BuildWise Server in production mode

   Run command *startup-production.bat* (or *startup.sh* on macOS/Linux) start the server.

3.4 Understand build working directories

The default working directory for BuildWise Demo Server (as the one we set up in Chapter 2) is `c:\agileway\.tmp\.buildwise` (`c:\agileway\.buildwise` *for production server*). You can find out the location of your BuildWise server on one project's setting page like below:

Edit project: AgileTravel Quick Build RSpec (agiletravel-quick-build-rspec)

Config file: *C:/agileway/tmp/.buildwise/config/agiletravel-quick-build-rspec.xml* (Show project config)

For every build project, BuildWise will create

- **a project setting file**

  `.buildwise/config/%PROJECT_ID%.xml`.

- **a working folder**

  `.buildwise/work/%PROJECT_ID%`.
  On the first build, a Git repository will be cloned from its parent (specified from project setup) to `sources` under the project's work folder.

Here is what it looks like:

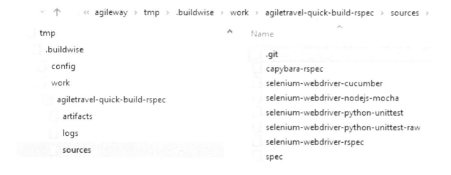

BuildWise will run test scripts under the '**sources**' folder.
(*if the* `.git` *folder is not shown, check the 'Hidden items' checkbox under Window Explorer's View tab*)

3.5 Exercise: Fix a failed build

We left an unfinished task in Chapter 2, the build was broken, now we will fix it. The build-fixing process is as below:

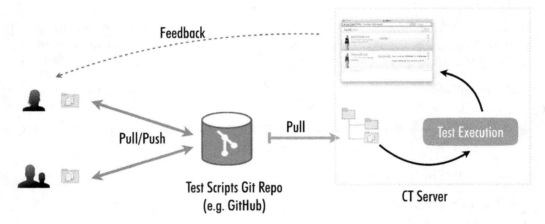

1. Identify the failed tests.

2. Fix the test failures locally.

3. Commit the changes and push up to the parent repository

4. Trigger another build and verify

5. Repeat 1 - 4 until gets a green build

Prerequisite: Make sure parent repository is writable

For our exercise, the parent repository is the one on Github. This is a private Git repository, which means not writable to you. A workaround is to change the working folder (under `.buildwise\work`) to another writable Git repository.

Open `.buildwise\work\agiletravel-quick-build-rspec\sources\.git\config` file in a text editor,

```
[remote "origin"]
        url = https://github.com/testwisely/agiletravel-ui-tests.git
        fetch = +refs/heads/*:refs/remotes/origin/*
```

change the `url` to our working folder: `C:\work\agiletravel-ui-tests`.

```
[remote "origin"]
        url = C:/work/agiletravel-ui-tests
        fetch = +refs/heads/*:refs/remotes/origin/*
```

 The purpose of showing this help you have a better understanding of how Git works.

Save the file. From now on, for a new build of this project, BuildWise will do a 'git pull' from `C:/work/agiletravel-ui-tests`.
For Windows users, please note the '/'.

Identify the failed tests

There was one failed test (shown on the build results page) in the last broken build.

⊙	TEST FILE (6 test cases in 4 test scripts files)	TIME (S)	RESULT ⌃
03-13 08:49	**03_passenger_spec.rb** 📄	8.8	
	- [4] Can enter passenger details (using page objects)	2.0	⚠ 📷

Click (the exclamation icon) to view the test output, which contains the failure message, and in which test step?

```
expected: "Wendi Tester"
     got: "Bob Tester"
(compared using ==)
./selenium-webdriver-rspec/spec/03_passenger_spec.rb:42:
```

and the screenshot of the web page when the failure occurred.

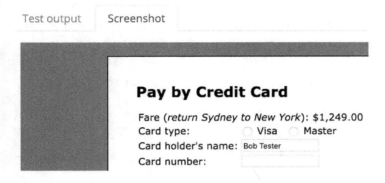

For the above, it is quite easy to know where the failure is.

Fix failed tests locally

Open the failed test (*passenger_spec.rb*) in TestWise and run the test case.

We got the same error like the one from the execution in BuildWise. That's good.

Once we identified the cause of test failures, fixing is usually easy and quick. In this case, just a simple change of the assertion text: Wendi → Bob. Rerun the test case locally (in TestWise or command line) until it passes.

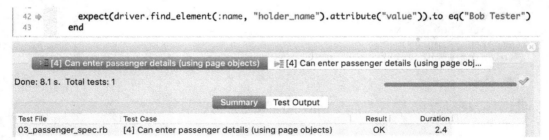

Commit the changes and push up to the parent repository

After we verified the fix, we commit the changes and push it up to the parent repository.

```
> cd C:\work\agiletravel-ui-tests
> git commit -am "fixed the assertion on passenger test"
```

Usually, we need to push the changes to the parent repository (`git push origin master`). But it is not needed for this exercise, as we 'hacked' the setup: the working directory is also the parent repository for the project (in BuildWise).

Trigger another build and verify

Immediately after `git push`, we trigger a build on BuildWise's web interface.

Shortly after a new build starts, you shall be able to verify the last checked-in message on the build page.

This means that BuildWise has got the latest changes (from Git) and is about to run the test suites again.

Monitor the test execution. When it completes, you shall get a green build.

3.6 Review

In this chapter, we examined how Continuous Testing works inside a BuildWise server. Despite the UI, all CI/CT servers fundamentally work the same way.

We have done an important exercise: fixing a broken build. A Continuous Testing engineer, as you can imagine, needs to do these many times a day. So please try to set up a CI server to get yourself familiar with this process.

In the next chapter, I will cover some non-hands-on topics. While hands-on is important (please keep doing that), understanding the whys and the hows are necessary as well. If someone is impressed with your work and asks you a few questions on CT, you will be able to answer them.

4. Why is CT important?

Being able to push out high-quality software releases frequently, without a doubt, is the most desirable outcome a software company wishes to have. The core process that enables frequent releases (with high quality) is Continuous Testing (CT in short). Thus, CT is the most important process of a highly efficient software team.

Some may wonder what are the exact benefits of CT. In Chapter 1, I briefly touched on a few of CT's benefits. After completing the exercise in Chapter 2, you have probably formed your own view on CT's benefits, such as

- enhancing product quality (by executing tests often)

- saving project cost (especially in terms of testing effort and resources)

- quick feedback

- being able to release to production frequently

These are the real benefits of CT, and there is so much more that it deserves its own chapter. Still, remembering I calling it *'the Holy Grail of software development'*? Once you have done a real Agile/DevOps project with a smooth CT pipeline, your understanding of software development will be changed completely.

In this chapter, I will skip the common CT benefits you might have heard from DevOps talks, and focus on the ones I learned from my own experiences.

4.1 Continuous Testing is the key to Agile

"In XP, testing is as important as programming" – Kent Beck, "Extreme Programming Explained", 2nd edition, page 102.

We all agree that the CT is the key practice of DevOps, as CT is directly reflected in the definition of DevOps. Please remember this, as there is a concerning trend of replacing the concept of DevOps with cloud deployment (using Docker or Kubernetes containers), which is wrong! DevOps engineers shall spend most of their efforts on ensuring reliable testing executions in a CT process.

CT is the key to Agile too. Back in early Agile days ($\sim$2004), core Agile practices included Continuous Integration, Automated Unit Testing, Refactoring and Pair programming. Functional test automation may or may not be implemented, because there was no reliable functional testing framework yet (until Watir came out in 2005). In the classic book "Extreme Programming Explained", Kent Beck (the father of Agile) dedicated a chapter on the "Toyota Production System" (Chapter 19). My understanding from reading that chapter: Continuous Testing.

With the wide adoption of Agile in recent years, the spirit of Agile has changed, unfortunately. Now we see more abstract practices known as Agile Ceremonies, such as "Planning meeting", "Story Estimation", "Retrospective" and "Burn Chart". However, from my observation these years, they brought bad reputations to Agile.

"Too much (agile) ceremony, ..., this is wrong", said by Father of Agile

"I was in South Africa, at Agile Africa, and somebody came up to me and said "Well, we want to do software development, but we just can't stand all this ceremony and Agile stuff. We just want to write some programs." And tears came into my eyes...like...how can it be that we who set out to refocus development on essentials and get rid of stuff that didn't matter, how can it be that we're right back where we were 20 years ago? Like how can it be that "this is too much ceremony"? ... No, this is wrong. I don't know what to do about it."

- Kent Beck, an interview in 2019[a]

[a]https://rackandstack-tech.blog/2019/10/15/kent-beck-fired-from-facebook/

In 2007, I led an Agile project with a strong focus on Continuous Testing. We did not have JIRA, 'Retrospective', 'Burn Chart' or long story estimation sessions. But we did have automated tests for 96% of user stories, and ran all the tests at least twice a day. Continuous Testing, unquestionably, was the heart of our development process. If we had a red lava lamp (connected to our build server to signal a broken build) for over a day, the manager would cancel any non-coding-or-testing activities, including daily standup meetings. Judging from the outcome of that project against the definition of DevOps, we have actually implemented DevOps. Back then, there was no such term, we were just doing Agile, a real one.

4.2 Detect regression errors quickly

"The only practical way to manage regression testing is to automate it." - Steve McConnell, "Code Complete" 2nd edition, page 528

Between 2010-2013, I spoke at a few international software testing conferences. Some conference organizers did a survey (before, during or after) of attendants' interested topics. From memories, the top ones always were (the order may change):

- Automated Testing

- Web app testing

- Regression testing

The interesting one is Regression testing. At one conference, after my talk, one attendant came up and said: "*I have attended many conferences, but your talk is the only one that really touched on regression testing with automation*". Knowing the attendants' interests in regression testing and test automation, I was quite surprised. How could that be? Since then, for every testing conference I went to, I looked for sessions on regression testing using automation. Sadly, no a single meaningful one.

If we talk about regression testing with any agile coach or project manager, they would say "regression testing is important". But do they really mean it? I have met one 'agile coach' who once said "*it is very important to use the Fibonacci sequence number to estimate your story points*", what a crazy idea! If everything is important, then nothing is important.

It is worth emphasising that regression testing is the most important type of software testing activity. Generally speaking, software customers have set quite low expectations on software quality (*remember the blue screen of death? When it happens, most people will just calmly reboot the machine*). From my experience, I think software customers are the most forgiving ones. They normally do not mind bugs or issues with new features. What they cannot tolerate when the existing features suddenly stop working after software updates. Regression testing prevents that from happening.

Due to the nature of software, regression issues happen often. One simple typo in code (e.g. an extra comma in JavaScript) may cause a number of web pages to be unusable. Furthermore, because the knowledge of code and business knowledge for broken features have already faded away in programmers' brains, programmers quite easily create more regression issues while fixing one.

Running automated functional tests as regression testing is the best way to prevent regression issues. It can keep your customers happy and your business safe.

4.3 Reduce/eliminate the needs for Defect Tracking

Defect tracking is a costly process. A senior project manager once told me that 15% of his whole project budget was spent on Defect Tracking and Triage (prioritizing defects based on severity, frequency and risk) processes. Quite often, I heard projects with hundreds of (at one extreme, over 1000) defects. Up to that stage, defect tracking is not helpful in fixing defects, isn't it? On the contrary, the process of defect tracking will not only consume your time and budget, but also create frustrations and anxiety.

Let me be clear, I do not like defect tracking. I will do my best to avoid it by eliminating the need for it. Believe it or not, after having worked on a real agile project (with comprehensive test automation), I found raising defects is unnatural in software development. (I could not remember the last time I raised a defect, while I have worked at a number of projects as a software testing engineer). Certainly, for the development of my own apps (since 2007), defect tracking was never used.

Let's examine why defect tracking is unhelpful and unnecessary:

- **Defect Tracking is an illusion**

  When a tester raises a defect, it does not mean that the defect will be fixed, nor a sure repeatable way to prevent that from happening. *I know some will argue about this, please read on.* It simply just created an illusion that this issue will be dealt with, which, again it is not guaranteed.

- **The steps to replicate the defect are quite often incorrect**

  The objective of software teams doing defect tracking is to record the steps that lead to a possible issue. However, it only works in theory. We, as humans, make a lot of mistakes in documenting a list of steps in an exact fashion.

  I once worked on a software testing project for a long-living system (over 20+ years). Its test design document (with written test steps and test data) was large and detailed, understandably, after years of revisions. However, a large percentage of test cases were simply not executable for newbies. Experienced testers were able to perform testing, mostly based on their past knowledge rather than the written test case design.

- **Promotes 'blaming culture'**

  How often have you heard of a programmer saying "*It worked on my machine*" or "*It is a feature, not a bug*"? I have worked as both a programmer and a tester. Therefore, I have seen countless debates on defects between programmers and testers, which brought inharmony to the team.

- **Inefficient tracking regression errors**

  High-risk features fail often. One regression issue may be detected many times during development. Do you raise the same defect multiple times or just one with a long list of notes? As you see, this complicates things.

- **When there are so many defects, tracking is meaningless**

  The tracking process will eat the team alive.

How to avoid these defect-tracking shenanigans? Simple, don't use it at all. When a defect is detected, replicate it in an automated test case. This new test joins existing tests as the regression testing suite, which will be run in a Continuous Testing process multiple times a day.

4.4 Try new ideas / upgrades

Modern software is commonly based on one framework, e.g. Ruby on Rails, and uses a number of third-party libraries. In other words, software has dependencies. A common approach to address this is library locking, such as 'Gemfile.lock' for Ruby on Rails and 'package.json' for Node.js. However, you do want to upgrade the software's underlying framework and its dependent libraries sometimes. How will you do it safely? Let me share a story:

Once I worked as a test manager on a government project based on the Microsoft SharePoint platform. In the middle of the development, the project manager was told to get our software to work on the newly released SharePoint 2009. He was clearly in panic, and had a few meetings with the architect and the program director on this. One day, he called a project meeting to discuss whether it was possible, and if so, what would be the impacts and efforts? I couldn't remember what the team members said, but the overall view was very pessimistic.

Then I said: "*It will be easy to find out. We have around 120 automated functional tests, which has reasonable coverage of our software features. If the developers could deploy our latest version into a SharePoint 2009 server, then I will run our automated tests against it to find out.*" The project manager breathed a sigh of relief, and decided to give it a go.

On the following day, I ran the test suite (with four build machines running concurrently) against the new platform. I did spend a few hours updating the test scripts, as identifications of some page elements changed. Because I used the maintainable test design (see my other book: Practical Web Test Automation[1]), I completed it within 4 hours. I sent the manager the test report, highlighting a handful of issues detected. It seemed to me that only minor development work was required. Developers worked based on the test report, check-in, regression testing in CT, ... Two days later, after getting a green build from our regression test suite, the development work resumed on the new platform.

4.5 CT is vital for the maintenance

The benefits of CT do not stop after the software is shipped (and accepted by the customer). Unless the software is on a rare once-off use purpose (e.g. Y2K problem), maintenance is required. The maintenance budget over its lifetime will usually be much bigger than the development cost.

While CT greatly boosts the team's productivity during the development phase, it shines even more during the maintenance phase. After the software is delivered, the development team will be dissembled, and the contractors moved on. The maintenance programmers are usually a different set of people who do not have good knowledge about the codebase (and its history). In other words, they are much more likely to introduce new defects while performing software updates or fixes.

A comprehensive automated functional test suite will provide the much-needed safety net for the poor maintenance team. With that, they could trigger a run of regression testing in CT server for every fix or update, to assure no new issues were introduced. As a matter of fact, the process is identical to how it was used during the development phase.

4.6 Training

According to a LinkedIn report[2], the software industry has the highest turnover rate of 13.2%. I call a new team member's first one or two weeks "write-off" time. Besides the usual machine set up and getting various access to systems, the new team member would spend most of his time on understanding the business and learning how to use the product. The team doesn't expect anything from a new team member during the 'write-off' time. Worse still,

---

[1]https://leanpub.com/practical-web-test-automation
[2]https://business.linkedin.com/talent-solutions/blog/trends-and-research/2018/the-3-industries-with-the-highest-turnover-rates

the manager needs to allocate existing members' time to help the new colleague. In my view, this cost may be largely saved with CT.

I usually created a folder `tutorial` under our functional tests folder. It may contain a set of test scripts for the typical workflows of the system. For example,

```
01_login_spec.rb
02_applicant_start_application_spec.rb
03_applicatn_lodge_applciation_spec.rb
04_manager_reivew_applciation_spec.rb
```

The test scripts were extracted from the existing functional tests, so it can be done quickly. A new team member may run these tests (in testing IDE such as TestWise) at his pace, repeat many times as necessary. Different from training videos, this execution is real (for web apps, running in a Chrome browser) on the new team member's machine. He may stop the execution at any time and explore the application.

If test scripts are written well, they shall be easy to read. Here is a tutorial script for "creating a group lesson on WhenWise booking".

```ruby
before(:all) do
  @driver = $driver = Selenium::WebDriver.for(browser_type, browser_options)
  @driver.navigate.to(site_url)
  reset
  sign_in("coach@biz.com")
end

it "Create a group lesson (tomorrow) on calendar" do
  visit("/calendar")
  calendar_page = CalendarPage.new(browser)
  calendar_page.click_next
  calendar_page.click_time_slot()

  calendar_new_modal_page = CalendarNewModalPage.new(browser)
  try_for(4, 2) { calendar_new_modal_page.click_training_class_tab }
  calendar_new_modal_page.enter_title("Monday Group Lesson")
  calendar_new_modal_page.enter_capacity("9")
  calendar_new_modal_page.enter_venue("City")
  calendar_new_modal_page.click_create

  calendar_page.click_event_with_title("Monday Group Lesson")
  calendar_lesson_modal_page = CalendarLessonModalPage.new(browser)
```

```
    try_for(2) { expect(calendar_lesson_modal_page.text).to include("Group lesson") }
  end
```

A new team member may follow the script to learn to use the application. As you can see, the test data is also present in the test script. By the way, the content of all test scripts can be visible via the CT server.

For those people who are not comfortable with testing tools, I have made these 'tutorial' scripts available on the BuildWise server. They could click to run a specific one in the browser (*we will cover this in later chapters*).

From my experience, this process greatly reduced the 'write-off' time and distraction to others.

4.7 Benefits for All Team Members

Continuous Testing is the heart of the software development process, it benefits all stakeholders of a software project.

Executives get financial rewards

The biggest beneficiary for a successful software product, financially speaking, is the owner and/or executives of the company. It is common knowledge that a good process of developing successful products is often more important than the products themselves. However, few software executives realize the full value of frequent pushing out software releases (multiple times per day), which is only possible with a good Continuous functional testing process in place.

It is easy for the executives to say "*we are going agile*", "*Steve Jobs once said ...*", blah, blah, blah. We know there is only one Steve Jobs (*who is known for being obsessed with quality. See his interview on quality*[3]). Most executives, instead, just want to keep the job, lacking a real desire to make a difference. As this Wired magazine's article[4] pointed out, LinkedIn '**completely overhauled**' its development and release process. Wow! However, if you think about it, it is so logical and it shall have always been like that. Engineering (in our process: software engineering, and in our titles: software engineers/testing engineers) shall mean something. In other industries, any serious business must have a repeatable process to ensure the product quality and the quality control process drives the production. Our software industry is the only exception.

---

[3]https://www.youtube.com/watch?v=kib6uXQsxBA
[4]https://www.wired.com/2013/04/linkedin-software-revolution/

> ## The software revolution behind LinkedIn's gushing profits [Wired]
>
> ..., It was Scott and his team of programmers who **completely overhauled** how LinkedIn develops and ships new updates to its website and apps, taking a system that required a full month to release new features and turning it into one that pushes out updates multiple times per day.
>
> ... Newly-added code is subjected to an elaborate series of **automated tests** designed to weed out any bugs.

In reality, most executives in the software industry are quite short-sighted. They usually possess leadership traits: high EQ, interpersonal skills, ..., etc. However, these are not enough for the software business, as it is quite different from others.

> "The top software developers are more productive than average software developers not by a factor of 10x or 100x or even 1,000x, but by 10,000x." – Nathan Myhrvold, the former Chief Technology Officer for Microsoft, quoted in "The 8th Habit: From Effectiveness to Greatness" by Stephen R. Covey

The real understanding of software development, for most people, can be only gained from years of testing and coding at a very high level. Of course, not everyone can be Mark Zuckerberg. A sensible way is to find a master software engineer (*not an easy task though*, like 'Kevin Scott was lured to LinkedIn') and follow his advice on engineering practices.

For all executives who have the ambition to make a difference, I recommend this insightful Forbes article: How Facebook Beat MySpace[5].

> ## A CEO talked high on test automation but acted low
>
> Once I worked on a medium-sized publicly-traded IT company, the new-hired CEO was planning to expand the software consulting business. He came to our Brisbane office and repeated a presentation he gave at a recent shareholder meeting. I was not in the office on that day. I heard the below from my colleagues.
>
> The CEO said:"*the reason that our software consulting division, with a high-profit margin, will succeed is that we have a world-leading test automation expert and access to state-of-*

---

[5]https://www.forbes.com/sites/adamhartung/2011/01/14/why-facebook-beat-myspace/#63d785bd147e

the-art test automation tools" (*He meant me and TestWise & BuildWise, heard from my manager*). The architect of our team raised his hand and asked: "*Zhimin is a contractor, what happens if he leaves?*". The CEO dodged the question.

A few weeks later, he visited the Brisbane office again, and came to shake hands with each staff. When I was introduced to him as '*the test automation guy*', he had no interest in seeing the test automation execution which was running on my computer at that time.

Several years later, I met a former colleague on the street. He told me that the software consulting business did not do well at all. The board sacked the CEO last month.

Managers can sleep well

Software managers deal with day-to-day software activities, as we know, it can be quite stressful. When a project starts, a manager usually refers to Project Management handbook for planning, risk assessment, ..., etc. A few weeks in the project, all that theoretic project management stuff would have been thrown away, as the project manager would be either in feel-like-endless meetings or consumed by putting out fires such as defects.

I have met a few project managers who believed that the project team should compromise quality to meet the deadline. This is very wrong, certainly in terms of general functional quality. (*non-functional maybe a different matter*)

Once I asked the audience during one presentation:

"*Which country or culture do you associate with the highest quality?*". "*Japan*" and "*Germany*" were the two answers from over 100 audiences.

My next question was "*Which country or culture do you associate with the highest efficiency?*", the answers were "*Japan*" and "*Germany*" again.

This experiment tells us that high efficiency comes from high quality. It is especially true for software development. For example, the widely-accepted code refactoring practice is a process of continuously refining the quality of the design (backed by automated testing) to improve ongoing development efficiency.

I once worked with a project manager, who had a programming background. He was impressed with my way of development: writing automated functional tests for each user story and keeping all regression tests pass by the end of the day. He pointed at the regression testing report on BuildWise, "*this makes me sleep well at night*".

Programmers get more efficient and satisfied

If I tell you that programmers, who work in an agile team, typically spend over 50% of their time on functional testing applications, you will probably be surprised. As a matter of fact, being a professional programmer for over 20 years, I would say 50% is a conservative figure. I have to admit that I only realized this after mastering real test automation, which I now see it so plain and obvious.

Let's examine how a programmer implements a new software feature (e.g. user story) for a web app.

1. Design

2. Write/debug code

3. Unit testing (only good programmers can really do this well)

4. Deploy to the local server instance

5. Verify the functions: open browser, log in a user, …, etc.

6. If find issues, go back to step 2.

Step 1 (Design) is usually quite light in agile teams. Among the four repetitive steps (2 - 5): two steps (3 and 5) are testing, Step 4 (Deployment to local server) shall be lightning-quick, therefore, its time is neglectable.

In the context of web applications, a lot of work involves tweaking CSS and JavaScript, which requires repeated verifications.

Now consider these:

- Quite commonly, it will take a few tries for a programmer to believe that he has got it right. For every try, he is actually conducting manual UI testing.

- Programmer demonstrates to a business analyst (or customer), who usually will find some issues or provide feedback. Back to Step 2, more manual testing.

- Another fellow programmer checked in some new code; A customer reported some regression issues. More manual testing.

- Requirement changes, as we know, are very common. When a feature is available on the test server, integration server or especially UAT server, requests for amendment can come at any stage. When that happens, programmers can get quite frustrated because he has most likely already started working on another user story. Now he needs to search the memory for things such as "what username should I use?" when testing the application manually.

There is more. Every showcase, release preparation and bug fix may involve a certain degree of manual demonstration/check as well.

Along with the development, more features will be added. This means, on the first sprint/iteration, a programmer's manual testing of a user story is usually quick, such as user login. The later ones will be longer and more boring as they often need to go through more steps.

Some programmers might disagree: "*I am not a tester, I am NOT performing against written-down test cases, only to check my work.*" Have you heard of 'exploratory testing', which opposites 'scripted testing'? The fact that you navigate the app to a certain state, choose login credentials such as 'manager01' and perform some checks, that's functional testing (= *test steps + test data + checks*). Dear programmers, unless you have mastered test automation (which is rare), you do a lot of manual testing every day.

Now we have established that programmers spend a lot of time on manual testing (*except top ones who mastered test automation. Still not a believer? I suggest you read books written by software legends such as Brian Kernighan, Kent Beck, Steve McConnell, Dave Thomas, Gerald Weinberg, Martin Fowler, ..., etc. pay special attention to the testing part*), then it will easier to see the great benefits of Continuous Testing can provide to programmers.

> ## My own productivity gain as a software developer
>
> Compared to myself, since I started practising test automation and continuous testing in 2005, my productivity (as a programmer producing software) is at least an order of magnitude better. Before 2007, I never imagined I would be able to develop my own software. Over the last 12 years, I have created
>
> - TestWise (functional testing IDE),
>
> - BuildWise (continuous testing server and agent),
>
> - ClinicWise (web-based clinic management system),
>
> - SiteWise (content management system) and

- WhenWise (services/resources booking app)

All development and support of the above were done in my spare time while I worked as an independent software testing and CI consultant. These software are well received by our customers. TestWise was a finalist in 2010 International Ruby award, and BuildWise won the 2nd prize of the Ruby Award in 2018.

My secret: test automation and continuous testing. Of course, there is more to it, but all are based on test automation. For example, writing/maintaining automated tests, in my view, is the best way to learn "keep design simple". Seasoned programmers would know that a "Simple and effective design" is extremely hard to achieve.

Testers have more fun

I have a lot of respect for testers, and I often worked as a hands-on tester. I gained a lot of insight into software design by working closely with testers as a consultant, programmer or mentor. I have to say, some bad manual testing processes that some organisations forced on the poor manual testers are just cruel. How could we say ourselves are doing High-Tech, if our testers spend most of their time doing this (in an Excel-like defect management system):

ID	Test Step	Result
1	Open the website	✓
2	Login with username 'john' and password 'letmein'	✓
3	Verify the dashboard is shown	✓
4	...	

Software testing can be done in a much more efficient, creative and fun way: test automation. In a recent project, I introduced test automation to the team and the manual testers (4 of them) were doing test automation with high spirits. In the farewell email from the lead developer who observed the changes, he wrote: "*I appreciate you giving our testers a new lease on life.*"

Two major concerns a manual tester has for test automation:

- **it is hard**

  Not really, it can be quite easy to get started. Both test automation and continuous testing can be learned in gradual steps. Under proper mentoring, testers may apply newly learned skills to work quickly. Most of the testers I mentored could develop a few automated test scripts for real work test cases, on the first day. You probably wouldn't believe that you could set up a CT server (from scratch) to run selenium tests within 30 minutes (the exercise in Chapter 2). Now you know it is possible.

- **it may replace my job**

  This is not true. Agile advocates more testing (naturally with more frequent releases) and automation. Compared to 10 years ago, I find there are usually more testers than programmers in an 'agile' team. Besides, the development of an automated test script starts with manual testing. I think manual testing, in exploratory testing form, is always needed. With continuous testing in place, testers might perform exploratory testing while a build is in progress.

  Furthermore, with repetitive and tedious regression testing having been taken care of largely by CT, testers now have time and tools (utilising testing scripts) to facilitate high-quality manual testing.

More importantly, for most manual testers, test automation brings joy to the work.

Business Analysts

Many people do not know that business analysts can also benefit from CT. Business analysts are those who manually use the application the most. Typically, a business analyst just wants to get a particular data scenario in the application. To achieve that, business analysts spend a lot of time using the application.

I once worked on an insurance claim application. Lodging a proper claim (with many different categories) could easily take 4 minutes even if every step is correct. After seeing that, I created a suite of automated scripts (in Selenium Ruby) to get newly lodged claim numbers for a few sets of scenarios, each taking 30 seconds on average.

One Business Analyst found out what I did, and loved it. Soon I received requests from all the business analysts for data, such as "*a claim on contents only*", "*home and content policy with over 1 million*", ..., etc. I extended the scripts and sent the claim numbers (from execution) back to them on Slack.

As this became a regular thing, I figured out a better way to let business analysts do it themselves. I created a special build project in BuildWise for BA, named "Data Generation for BA". A business analyst can click a button to trigger a build, she may move on to other tasks such as having a coffee, then get the desired data from BuildWise. Furthermore, team members may run an individual script to get a specific type of data quickly.

To give a feel on how well this was received by the business analysts, here is a follow-up story. A year after at a different organisation, I was introduced to another project team (not mine). One business analyst (from the last project) saw me, she immediately said to her project manager: "*Can we get Zhimin to work with us?*"

Boost Customer's confidence

"On-site Customer" is one of the agile practices, it is a pity that this practice seemed to have been forgotten in recent years. Besides human factors, I think the main reason is the low productivity caused by fake agile ceremonies. It is not practical to ask an on-site customer to wait 9 working days (*a typical sprint length is 2 weeks, which I think is too long. I recommend 2 sprints per week, if CT is implemented, it is not hard to achieve at all*) to get his hands on trying out the application.

The customers care only about the product. Most on-site customers would not like to be involved with those non-sense agile ceremonies. Imagine you are a customer representative who is assigned to work with the software team. You take time out of your normal work to attend a number of meetings talking about story points, velocity and burn charts in JIRA. You would be pissed off too.

Take showcases as an example. A showcase is a gathering of the software team to show what business functions they have accomplished, and demonstrated them to the customer for feedback. However, over the years, I have noticed showcases have gradually changed to focus more on talking, rather than showing. The showcase meeting has become dull and boring. Every single time, when I ran automated tests against the real server, I could feel the atmosphere in the meeting room became live. The real stuff is what people want to see.

I remember one particular showcase done by one customer representative. You read it right, the customer demonstrated newly-implemented features in the showcase. Thanks to our CT process, the team rolled out features quickly, and most of the customer's feedback was addressed within 2 days. Naturally, the customer involved more. She saw the test executions in the CT server (BuildWise) and even ran specific tests sometimes in testing IDE (TestWise). In one showcase, after she demonstrated the new features implemented in the sprint, she said: "*This is a new important feature we are also working on, coming in the next sprint ....*". She demonstrated a few steps, an error occurred (with the error stack trace shown in red on the screen). She was still smiling: "As I said, *this is a work-in-progress, the guys will fix this.*" Tim, the developer who worked on this new feature, was busy noting this down (*he probably could not wait to add an automated test to replicate the error*).

What impressed me the most was that, when that error occurred, the atmosphere in the room was still relaxed. Because we all knew, including the customer, the error would be captured in a new automated test, and it would not happen again.

Regularly showing business features via automation will boost the customer's confidence in the product. Its benefits are hard to quantify. On another project, we used test automation and CT regularly in the showcases. Later during the warranty period, the CIO of the customer said to our project manager: "*Send me a BuildWise report of a green build, then you have my permission to deploy the update to the production*".

4.8 Review

This was a long chapter, there are still many other benefits of CT and I still have more stories to share. I realize that readers might already feel overwhelmed and I've got to stop somewhere.

I hope you have been practising CT at work or in your spare time. In the next chapter, we will go back to the hands-on stuff.

5. Set up your own build project

In Chapter 2, we configured a sample project in the BuildWise server to run some Selenium tests. It was done quickly to just give readers a feel of test execution in a CT server. I understand some readers might not be convinced yet, want to see executions of their tests. In this chapter, I will show how to set up a BuildWise project to run your own tests, step by step.

Please note that while the instructions are specific to BuildWise, these procedures are generic. You will find it easy to apply most CI/CT servers.

5.1 Prepare your test scripts

Prerequisite

- Basic knowledge of using Git from the command line

- Your tests are executable from the command line

Objective

Test scripts in a Git repository.

Action

1. Create automated tests for your site

   Create a few test scripts for a website you are familiar with, in one of these **RSpec**, **Pytest**, **Mocha** and **Cucumber** test syntax. The test scripts and associated files shall be in a folder, e.g. `c:\work\project-ui-tests`.

   If you are new to test automation, I suggest using TestWise IDE to create the test project skeleton, which contains the build scripts for BuildWise. If you have existing test scripts, you may copy the following files from a sample project[1].

---

[1]https://github.com/testwisely/agiletravel-ui-tests

- buildwise.rake
- buildwise_rspec_formatter.rb
- Rakefile
- spec/spec_helper.rb

2. Verify test execution from the command line, as below

```
> cd c:\work\project-ui-tests\spec
> rspec login_spec.rb
```

3. Verify invoking a build target from the command line

```
> cd c:\work\project-ui-tests
> rake -f Rakefile ui_tests:quick
```

Note: `ui_tests:quick` is a sample build target (to run a set of RSpec tests) defined in the sample `Rakefile`. If you get '*An error occurred while loading spec_helper*', make sure `spec/spec_helper.rb` is present.

4. Add to the version control (if not done already)

```
> cd c:\work\project-ui-tests
> git add .
> git commit -am "initial version"
```

5. Set up the parent repository (if not set already)

The `C:\work\project-ui-tests` is a local Git repository, we need a parent repository (shared among the team). Github or Bitbucket are commonly used as the team repository in large organisations. For simplicity, I will use a network folder (`G:\repos`) as the team repository.

Create a git repository on a shared folder.

```
> cd G:\repos
> git init
```

Set the `G:\repos` as the parent repository.

```
> git remote add origin G:\repos
> git push origin master
```

5.2 Create a new build project

Objective

Set up a build configuration in BuildWise so that we can trigger a run of tests with a click of a button.

Information

A build configuration is called a project in BuildWise. We may (and often we do) create multiple build projects for the same test script repository, such as executing several key tests or all tests in parallel.

The key data needed for creating a new build project:

- **Project Name and Identifier**

  For identification purposes.

- **Working folder**

  The absolute path of the working test script folder, e.g. `c:/work/project-ui-tests`

- **UI test folder**

  The relative path to the working folder, e.g. `spec`.

- **Rake task name for UI or API Testing**

  The task that executes a set of functional tests. The default task name is `ci:ui_-tests:quick`. (*we will cover build tasks in a later chapter*)

Action

Click "New Project" link.

Enter the project name, working folder path, UI test folder and test execution task.

New project

Option 1. Loading from a working folder or Specify manually   Fill demo project ▾

Project name:	My UI Tests	
Identifier:	my-ui-tests	*(lower case and unique, e.g. clinicwise-ui-tests)*
Working folder:	c:\work\project-ui-tests	
UI test folder:			
Test results folder:	relative path, e.g. spec/reports	
Rake task for UI or API Testing:	ci:ui_tests:quick	UI test framework: RSpec (Ruby) ▾

Create   Cancel

Click "**Create**" button.

Test execution task definition

The `ci:ui_tests:quick` is a build task name that invokes test execution. If you created the project in TestWise, the build task is already included with the following files (included as a part of TestWise project template).

- `buildwise.rake`

- `Rakefile`

- `buildwise_rspec_formatter.rb`

If not, you can copy the above files from a sample project.

Do not worry about the actual definition of this build task yet. We will study it in Chapter 7.

5.3 Trigger a build manually

Objective

To run a set of automated tests.

Information

When the application is ready (for testing), you can trigger a run (which I often refer to it as a build).

 There is no built-in support for scheduled (time-based) and post-commit hooks in BuildWise, because I discourage these practices. If you are desperate, you can implement them quite easily via BuildWise API.

Action

Click "**Build Now**" button.

 AgileTravel Quick Build RSpec 📈

NEVER BUILT

Build Now

5.4 View a build in progress

After a build started, you will be redirected to the build page, where you can view the build progress. (if not, click the blue 'XX:building' link)

5.5 Cancel a build

Objective

Stop the currently running build.

      BuildWise only allows one active build at a time.

Action

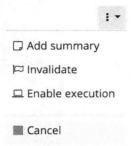

□ Add summary

⚑ Invalidate

💻 Enable execution

■ Cancel

5.6 View Change Log

Objective

Find out who changed what, from Git commit history.

 BuildWise shows all the commits since the last successful run.

Action

On the build page, click '**Git Pull**' on the left.

5.7 Build history

Objective

View the history of the builds for one project.

Action

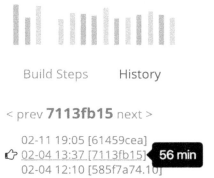

5.8 View test failures and screenshot

When tests fail (which will happen often), naturally, we would like to quickly find out the cause of it. While we can only be certain when we rerun the failed test (in testing IDE), a quick view of the test output and the screenshot (if applicable) will be helpful.

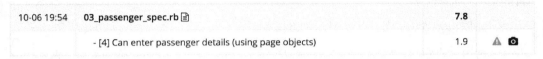

Click the exclamation icon to view the test output.

Click the camera icon to view the screenshot of the browser window when the failure occurred.

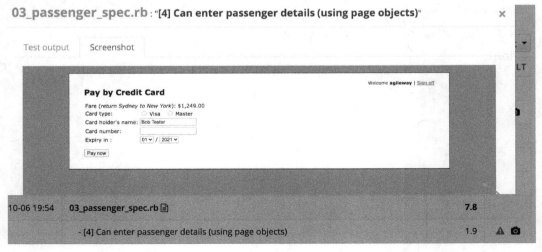

5.9 View test script content

Objective

View the content of a test script. This can be useful for the team members to review the test script directly in their browsers.

Action

Click the file icon on the right of the test script file.

12-30 16:45   **01_login_spec.rb** 📄 Output

Show test script

- [1] Can sign in OK

- [1] User failed to sign in due to invalid password

The syntax-highlighted test script will be shown in a popup window.

```
01_login_spec.rb                                                           ×

 1  load File.dirname(__FILE__) + '/../test_helper.rb'
 2
 3  describe "User Login" do
 4    include TestHelper
 5
 6    before(:all) do
 7      # for windows, when unable auto-detect firefox binary
 8      # Please note Firefox on 32 bit is "C:\Program Files (x86)\Mozilla Firefox\firefo
 9      # Selenium::WebDriver::Firefox::Binary.path="C:/Program Files/Mozilla Firefox/fir
10
11      @driver = $browser = Selenium::WebDriver.for(browser_type, browser_options)
12      driver.manage().window().resize_to(1280, 720)
13      driver.manage().window().move_to(30, 78)
14      driver.get(site_url)
15
16      driver.navigate.to(site_url)
17    end
18
19    after(:all) do
20      driver.quit unless debugging?
21    end
22
23    it "[1] Can sign in OK" do
24      goto_page("/login")
25      login_page = LoginPage.new(driver)
26      login_page.login("agileway", "testwise")
27      # selenium does not have browser.text yet
28      try_for(3) { expect(driver.page_source).to include("Welcome")}
29      driver.find_element(:link_text, "Sign off").click
30      puts "[stdout] Signed out"
31    end
32
33    it "[1] User failed to sign in due to invalid password", :tag => "showcase" do
34      goto_page("/login")
35      login_page = LoginPage.new(driver)
36      login_page.login("agileway", "badpass")
37      expect(driver.page_source).to include("Invalid email or password")
38    end
39
```

5.10 View test execution history

Objective

Find out the execution history of a particular test script. When a test failed, the history graph (like the one below) can help to narrow down when a possible break was introduced.

Action

Click the file name of a test script to view its execution history.

group_lesson_book_spec.rb   ✕

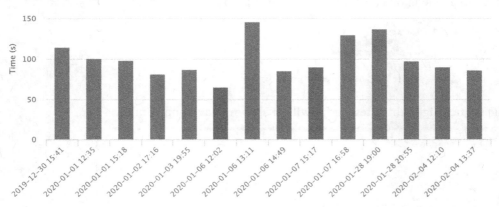

5.11 Build report

The build report comes with filtering and sorting. You may export to other formats such as Excel.

● UI Test Results (6 tests)

Filter by test case name, test script file name 🔍   Export ▼

⊙	TEST FILE (6 test cases in 4 test scripts files)		
		Excel	
10-19 19:51	01_login_spec.rb 📄 Output	CSV	
	- [1] Can sign in OK		
	- [1] User failed to sign in due to invalid password	Print to PDF	
10-19 19:51	02_flight_spec.rb 📄	8.8	
	- [3] Return trip	2.3	OK
	- [2] One-way trip	2.1	OK
10-19 19:51	03_passenger_spec.rb 📄	7.0	
	- [4] Can enter passenger details (using page objects)	1.8	OK
10-19 19:51	04_payment_spec.rb 📄 Output	14.0	
	booking number: 13103		
	- [5] Book flight with payment	9.6	OK

6. How to succeed in CT?

Continuous Testing requires a high standard of pretty much everything because it runs hundreds of automated end-to-end tests daily. Just name a few:

- Reliable Test framework

- Solid and fast server environments

- Fast and reliable build and deployment process

- High-quality automated test scripts

- Repeatable test data

- ...

In this chapter, let's see what it takes to succeed in CT: the Holy Grail of software development.

6.1 Definition of Success: AgileWay CT Grading

Many fake Agile/DevOps consulting companies provide dubious CT practices, one main reason is that we lack a good grading system to expose them. There are some DevOps maturity models, however, they seemed too abstract to me. As we know, 'talkers' are good at making things abstract, hence, difficult to assess. In view of this, I have created an easy-to-assess grading system and named it "AgileWay CT Grading".

Objective

To be able to assess the level of CT in a software project, instantly.

Assumptions

- Each automated functional test is at the user-story scenario level

- All tests are executed for each CT run

- No human intervention at all during the course of test execution

- When software changes, automated regression testing is performed

If any of the above is not met, Level **0**.

AgileWay Continuous Testing Grading Table

Level	Criteria (E2E test count)	Action
0	< 20	Seek help or give up immediately
1	20	Seek help if struggling to maintain all tests
2	50	Keep running daily. Change any process/tool to grow further. Seek help if necessary
3	200	Improve parallel testing, data reset
4	500	Scale test lab and more efficient Server-Agents communication
5	1000	Be happy there, growing further requires much larger investment
6	5000+	Be aware of new competitors who embrace CT

There is no scientific base for this, purely based on my experience and observation (for over 14 years). Discard it if you don't like it.

My estimated achievement rates of each level.

Level	Achievement rate in Industry	Notes
0	~50%	*Fake Agile if the situation lasts over 1 week*
1	~40%	*Fake DevOps if not running every day*
2	~9%	*The team see the benefits*
3	~0.9%	*Real Agile*
4	~0.09%	*Real DevOps, release daily*
5	~0.009%	*World Class*
6	a handful in the world	*Facebook/Google level*

I understand that some will disagree with my estimates (especially on the achievement rates). I suggest you get a pencil and fill the table below.

	Assessment Question	Current Project	Previous	... ...
1	Has user-story-level automated functional tests?	Y / N	Y / N	
2	All tests executed in a CT/CI server?	Y / N	Y / N	
3	How often do you run them?	daily/weekly	daily/weekly	
4	Get a green build (all tests pass) every day?	Y / N	Y / N	
5	Test count	_____	_____	
	LEVEL SCORE:			
	(0 if the answer for #1 - #4 is not the first option)	_____	_____	

My guess would be, like most of the people who have done these exercises in my training (or mentoring) sessions, **Level 0** for all projects.

My Score

I know your next question to me will be: "*which level are you in then?*" My answer is **Level 4**. The below are the UI test counts (as of 2021-09-22) for my three apps, which I push new builds to the production as long as the regression tests pass in our CT server (BuildWise).

App name	App Type	Regression (UI) test suite	in CT	Total executions
ClinicWise	Web app	**611** Selenium WebDriver	7+ years	618,549
TestWise IDE	Desktop app	**304** Appium	2+ years	63,043
WhenWise	PWA	**548** Selenium WebDriver	3 years	332,389

(*For experienced CT engineers, the total number of test executions might seem low. This is because I develop and maintain these 3 apps mostly in my spare time*)

I helped to implement CT for a number of clients, which I won't share here. What I can tell you is that a large percent of the projects reached **Level 3**.

6.2 Functional test automation and continuous execution are interdependent

Below are the six stages of a failed test automation/CT attempt, which I have seen too many over the last 13 years.

1. A new CIO's proposal or Agile/DevOps movement starts a Proof of Concept (POC)

   "*It takes 2-month to do a buggy release, the testing process is costly and ineffective, we must do something*". The answer is usually "Test Automation" and "CI/CD".

2. A hero infrastructure engineer set up successful execution of an automated functional test (in Cucumber or others)

The POC is working, everyone was excited.

3. More test scripts check-in, getting a green build (all tests pass) is increasing hard

    Infrastructure engineers trigger builds more often in hope to get a green build.

4. Soon, it is becoming impossible to get a green build

    Many old tests fail, and infrastructure engineers have lost faith. All parties involved distant themselves with CI/CD.

5. Very high test failures in each build

    "50%+ tests failed" and "Last success was 3 months ago" on the CI server's build page. Ironically, those out-of-date tests were still triggered to run in the CI server every day, but no one cares anymore.

6. Give up

    Find a scapegoat to blame. After a period of quiet time, someone proposes "maybe another test framework will work?", back to Stage 1.

The biggest reason for many CT failures, in my opinion, is that the executives lack the understanding of the relationship between functional test automation and continuous execution. Commonly, the test automation engineers in individual software projects develop automated test scripts, then pass to the infrastructure team to run them. This is wrong!

In this model (the left in the above graph), test automation engineers have little exposure to how their tests were executed, and infrastructure engineers have little knowledge of the test scripts.

The correct model (the right in the diagram) is that functional test automation and continuous execution are tightly coupled. Real CT is only possible if both two work well together.

- CI/CD/CT has no much value if not running E2E functional tests

  For many software projects, the realised contributions of using a CI server are limited to building a software package, and maybe executing some unit tests. It is common. However, what about "Integration" or "Delivery" in CI/CD? The purpose of CI/CD/CT is to produce a quality release candidate after it has been thoroughly tested. If there were test failures, feedback is provided to the team to investigate. If we CI/CD in the context of the actual delivery (to production), executions of a comprehensive E2E functional test suite is a must.

- CT complements Functional Test Automation

  Compared to unit tests execution of automated functional tests is slow and brittle. A good CT process can mediate that. *(will be covered in later chapters)*

- Continuous Execution affects how functional tests are designed

  The design of automated test scripts is largely dependent on how they are going to be executed. For example, running two tests concurrently with one deleting the user 'test01' and the other logging in as 'test01' won't work well.

- Maintenace of Functional Test Automation requires tests to be run frequently

  Test script creation is only a minor effort compared to ongoing test refinement and maintenance, which require lots of executions (maybe on different dates or time). It is practically impossible to run all functional tests often on one engineer's local machine.

For any organisation, finding a real CT engineer who has hands-on expertise in both test automation and continuous execution is not easy. But a wise IT executive will learn from past mistakes and get the culture ready. Quite often, the correct approach in CT is more intuitive, immediately effective and cost-saving. For example, a good approach to implement the right mode is to **let individual teams set up and maintain their own CT infrastructure**. Readers of this book know how quickly they can set up one.

9 months of trying to run automated UI tests in a CI server!

In 2019, at one large company, I was shocked to hear that the Agile Transformation team has been trying to get sample automated tests (UFT) running in a CI server (Bamboo). This is a classic example of test automation and Continuous Execution being worked in isolation. The test architects in the Agile Transformation team decided on the test framework; the infrastructure architects (in the same team) decided on the CI server (but known as 'deployment server' in the company). This debacle has nothing to do with a specific test framework or CI server, it is a failure of IT leadership. How could let it happen for so long?

Here I point out a simple fact: the knowledge and experience of executing automated UI tests for web apps in CT are mostly transferable across projects and companies.

6.3 Success Factors (test automation)

The prerequisite of CT is a solid test automation solution with easy-to-maintain test scripts that can execute reliably.

Solid Test Automation Framework

The foundation of CT is functional test automation. If the underlying test framework is fragile, doing CT will be a total waste of time.

The choice of the test framework is quite easy now. Since 2016, Microsoft has started deprecating its own testing tool Coded UI with the following recommendations[1]: "With the WebDriver becoming a W3C standard, we are actively encouraging customers to use Selenium for web-apps and with the WinAppDriver becoming available for Windows apps, to use Appium for Windows apps."

I agree with Microsoft's recommendation.

App type	recommended automation framework
Web app	Selenium WebDriver
Desktop app	Appium + WinAppDriver
Mobile app	Appium + iOSDriver/Android Driver
API	Raw script language

Test script in a scripting language

A standard automation framework is usually available in several programming languages. For example, Selenium WebDriver's official languages are Ruby, Python, Java, JavaScript and

---

[1]https://devblogs.microsoft.com/devops/visual-studio-team-services-testing-tools-roadmap/#SeleniumAppium

C#. A common mistake is to use the team's development language (such as Java and C#) to script automated tests. The simple reason is that **test scripts shall be written in a scripting language**.

My recommendation for a test scripting language is Ruby. There is a lot of greatness of Ruby that makes it ideal for scripting test automation. The modern UI test automation started from Watir, its creators loved Ruby so much that they put Ruby in the name of the framework: Web Application Testing in Ruby.

Reliable individual test execution

This is about the quality of test scripts. If the stability of individual test execution is not high, forget about Continuous Testing. Remember, a green build is to pass all tests!

	1 test		75 tests	
Average pass rate for 1 test	**90%**	→	0.04%	Chance of getting a green build
	99%	→	47.1%	
	99.9%	→	92.8%	

There may be a number of reasons for unreliable tests, just name a few below:

- Does it run at the beginning of the month, or on December 31st?

- Will one test execution affect another?

- Special date, e.g. 29th of February

- Special time, e.g. local time of GMT 12AM date

Maintain test script with high efficiency

Continuous Testing means continuous maintenance of test scripts. High efficiency is required, as we are dealing with all test scripts (from Sprint 1) of every build in the CT server.

The test scripts shall follow maintainable test design and you shall use your testing tools efficiently. Refer to my other book 'Practical Web Test Automaton' for these topics.

Freedom

Given Selenium WebDriver is a W3C standard, free and reliable, you would assume that there shall be no room for vendor-locking test automation framework or tools. Sadly, a large percentage of projects I visited purchased one or more vendor-locking testing tools. Not surprisingly, these projects all failed.

Vendor locking is bad, as it leads to many problems, such as

- missing features (not supported by browser vendors who only supports WebDriver)

- unreliable test execution (one reason: not based on W3C standard)

- very limited help from Stack Overflow

- not flexible (comparing to direct use of scripting language)

- runtime license may be required even for test execution

Affordable

In the true spirit of DevOps, every member of a software team may utilize automated functional tests. From my experience, CT works better when all team members use the same testing tool.

The rise of Selenium WebDriver makes UI test automation for web apps is available to all software teams, as it is free. Before that, you would look at around US$10,000 per license for a testing automation tool, which did not even work well at all (the fact: they were gradually fading out). By choosing a correct framework, such as Selenium WebDriver, you don't need to worry about the cost.

6.4 Success Factors (infrastructure)

The infrastructure currently being used for manual testing won't be enough for CT.

Reliable server infrastructure

Functional Testing, regardless of automated or not, is to verify the functionality of an application deployed in a server environment. If the target server environment is not reliable, for example, the connection between the app server and the database server is flaky, it will impact the test execution.

Continuous Testing makes the server infrastructure problems more apparent for the following two reasons:

- Load

  Test executions triggered in CT server will generate a lot more load on the target application server.

- Objective

  The result of automated test execution is either a success or a failure.

Some software projects used the excuse of "Continuous Testing is too hard" for their failure was not totally fair, as the server infrastructure was simply not ready it.

Rapid, reliable and repeatable deployment

We want to run the automated test suite frequently, to detect regression issues. If one regression issue is detected, and the team has a good defect-fixing process as below:

- feedback is sent to the development team

- a programmer found the cause (and verified with the assistance of the automated test)

- a fix is checked in

- a new build is triggered on CI server and deployment artifacts were generated

The programmers and the testers would be eager to confirm whether this new build fixed the issue, and more importantly, not break the existing functionalities. Now, imagine that the deployment has to wait for one particular deployment engineer John to work on his magic (including tweaking numerous settings manually) for 30 minutes, the continuous testing process simply won't work well.

Dedicated test lab

To run a large test functional test suite, parallel execution is the only practical way to provide quick feedback. As we know, feedback is important in CT, as in any pipeline.

With the advancement of VM technologies and cloud-based deployment, the cost of setting up a dedicated functional testing lab is low. As a matter of fact, I commonly set up one within an hour on my first day of consulting: 3 VMs on a laptop computer. Starting small, growing as necessary.

6.5 Success Factors (continuous execution)

Compared to unit tests, the execution of functional tests is more brittle and takes much longer. Hence, traditional CI servers are not capable of meeting the challenge.

Low false alarm rate

A false alarm in CT means a deceptive or erroneous report of a test failure, causing unnecessary panic. False alarms in CT are inevitable. However, if the false alarm rate is high, the team (especially the programmers) will lose trust in the CT process. When that happens, CT will fail.

Quick Feedback

Programmers may use techniques such as Mocks and in-memory database to speed up the execution. However, we can do little to speed up the execution of an automated UI test, at the **individual** level. We can provide '**quicker**' feedback at the test suite level.

- Reduce overall execution time by parallel execution

  If the average test execution time is 1 minute, the total execution time of 100-test will be 100 minutes. If we run them in a parallel testing lab with 10 agents. The expected overall execution time will be around 15 minutes (after factoring in the overhead), a saving of 85%!

- Run recent failed test first

  After fixing one test failure (either the code or the test script), we want to see it run in CT immediately. In other words, we'd like to see this one to be run first in the CT build. If it is failed again, we can start investigating right away while the build is still in progress.

Scalable with parallel test execution

Parallel execution is the only practical way to manage the execution of a large suite of automated UI tests. The parallel execution is a must-have feature of CT servers.

Auto retry

UI test execution, by nature, is brittle. For a suite of 75 UI tests with an average of 99% execution reliability for an individual test, only 47% chance to have a successful build. This is a simple probability in maths.

The solution is actually simple, by using the same principle of Probability in a reverse manner: Auto-Retry. That is, if a test failed on one Agent, CT server automatically gives it another chance by running it on another agent. This greatly reduces false alarms.

Same testing tool for the whole team

The test scripts belong to the team, i.e., every team member may run and edit test scripts. When debugging test failures in CT (very often), the team need to act quickly. It is important that the team share the same understanding of test scripts in terms of the design and conventions. Thus, using the same testing tool can help improve efficiency and avoid confusion.

6.6 Success Factors (human)

Software development is essentially human activity. The human factors play an important role in whether the software will be successful in test automation and CT. The fact is that most executives, managers and tech leads do not have the knowledge of CI, and never have any successful experience. The nature of CT is to provide feedback. If the management is really keen to learn and courageous to act on the feedback, the journey to CT will be much easier.

Realize on-going efforts (executives)

The words 'regression' and 'continuous' in CT mean the on-going repeated work. In reality, most executives throw millions of dollars to form a team (often called 'Agile Transformation' or 'DevOps' team) to implement CT. If the team can come up with one demonstration, it was considered successful. When the practices were introduced into a real project, the issues start to show up after a few sprints, such as

- Hard to keep the test scripts up to date with application changes

- Test execution is not reliable

- Reusable test data

- Pass rate of test execution in CI keeps dropping

- ...

Does it sound familiar? The reason is simple, the company is not really serious about CT. When it is reflected at the management level, project managers tend to plan 'test automation' (creating a story card in JIRA). When an automated test is created, run once, the task (or user story card) is marked done. This is wrong.

In my opinion, test creation only counts for around 10% of the efforts during the life cycle of one automated test. The other two phases: test stabilising/refinement and test maintenance count for around 30% and 60%, respectively.

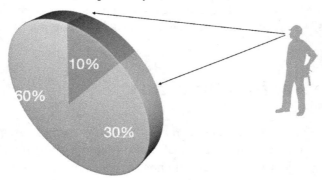

Unfortunately, most IT managers only appreciate the efforts of test creation and minor parts of test maintenance. After all, in a company that favours useless burn charts, it would be silly for a manager to create long-running story cards for test maintenance. When the harder work was not on JIRA board, who is willing to do it? No wonder test automation and CT attempts kept failing in many organisations.

"At Agileway, while we don't do time-recording, we estimated 70+% efforts (of all SDLC activities) were spent on CT. In return, we get 10x more productivity (compared to ourselves). This is our secret for creating several large software such as TestWise, BuildWise, ClinicWise and WhenWise. Each of these software will take 10 times more manpower in a company than in ours." – Zhimin Zhan

Why Google and Facebook do so well in CT? Because their CEOs are first-class programmers. They know the importance of CT from their hands-on experiences. This realization, of course, can be learnt by changing the mindset, quickly. I have seen 'Transform to Agile Delivery Model" movements in a few large organisations, though the changes were only superficial. CT makes Agile real and DevOps possible, and exposes shortcomings of all phases of software development activities. An experienced IT executive shall know how much resistance he is going to face.

So, if you are an IT executive who wants to implement a successful CT for once, do it real. Make CT the top priority work item, daily.

Open mindset and judge objectively (tech leads)

With over 13 years of consulting in CT, I found the middle-tech-tiers (with titles such as Test Architect, Technical Architect, Tech Lead, Principal software engineer, .., etc) often the blockers. For some, it seemed to be their interests for CT to fail, for the following reasons:

- Lack of knowledge

  The fact of the CT is not running shows the middle-tech-tiers do not have the knowledge that would make CT work. Please note, functional test automation and CT knowledge are fully transferable between jobs.

- Fear of changes and unknowns

  In 2011, LinkedIn completed changed how they develop software under the guidance of Kevin Scott, who was "lured" from Google. Generally speaking, most people do not like changes, especially those that could affect how they work or even job safety.

- Recommended wrong test automation tools

  Commonly, they had recommended the wrong test automation framework/tools. Or worse, they "designed a test framework" and then failed. These past experiences made them hard to accept the proper one: raw Selenium WebDriver, which is free and open-source.

- Fear of new technologies

  The middle-tech-tier engineers tend to spend more time on all kinds of meetings, rather than hands-on stuff. Gradually, they are fixated with technologies that they were comfortable with. For example, Java (as a compiled language) is not suitable for scripting automated tests. If this tech lead only knows Java well, he will most probably vote no to a good solution in Ruby that a real CT engineer presented.

Having said that, I did meet some good engineers who were keen to learn and grow, I have high respect for them. The lack of knowledge in test automation and CT is not their faults. It is due to the failure of IT education and leadership.

How to make tech-leads embrace CT?

A competent executive can turn the things around and get the middle-tech-tiers to work towards the goal.

- A firm message to implement CT

  Something like "*All new projects must have CT in place, as daily deployment to the production will be mandatory*". This will make people think and do out of their comfort zones.

- Start with one project, then roll out company-wide gradually

  It is far easier to implement just one project first with a new process. Once it is done successfully, applying to others will be easy.

- Create incentives for the engineering team

  Reward engineers who work on test automation and CT. They deserve that as they are doing harder and far more valuable work than normal coders.

- Introducing test automation and CT mentor

  A competent mentor brings years of experiences, a quick and most cost-effective way to not only getting things done but also training the staff. Furthermore, mentors will leave after the job done, no threats to engineers' jobs.

- make all engineers follow test automation mentor's tech advice unconditionally

  Get them into a learning mode. It is common (and easy) that a middle-tech-tier engineer comes up with excuses, a typical one is "*that will never work in our company*". I trained many engineers, most of Java programmers usually showed no interests in learning Ruby at the beginning of the first day. For some who did spend a day learning, they loved Ruby and some even thanked me for it.

Access to a good test automation & CT mentor

Comparing to other types of consulting in the software industry, test automation and CT coaching is probably the most effective and economical one. An experienced test automation coach can answer your specific questions within hours, sometimes even in minutes, as they can analyze the problem without the need to understand how the software was designed. The knowledge they have gained from other projects can often be applied to yours directly, thus saving you days/months of non-productive (or worse, counter-productive) efforts. Test script files are generally very small, so that they can be easily exchanged between the team and the coach. This avoids misunderstandings. Furthermore, if possible, you can even give the test coach access to your public test site, so he or she can better help you by running the test scripts remotely.

Some may wonder: how can we find a good test automation and CT mentor? First of all, you need to know what to look for, otherwise easily fall into the fake ones.

 A good test automation and CT coach shall be able to create a couple of key E2E automated tests and set up a CT server to run them, all in **one day**.

Don't waste the time of advertising a role on a job-seeking site. Good test automation and CT engineers are usually in big demand (*remembering LinkedIn needed to lure Kevin Scott from Google*), they won't be interested in a permanent position. Instead, I recommend you directly contact the renowned experts, book authors and the engineers of open-source projects. Also, don't limit the search within your city and country. Now that people are comfortable working remotely via video-conferencing software such as Zoom, getting the best people in the world to help you is possible and often more affordable than you think.

Deploy on green builds

"Practices should lower stress. An automated build becomes a stress reliever at a crunch time. 'Did we make a mistake? Let's just build and see'." - Kent Beck (Extreme Programming Explained 2nd edition, 2005, p. 49).

The "Release early, release often" slogan has been used by many software projects. When do you push a new release build to the production server? The answer is "immediately after getting a green build in CT", i.e, passing all automated user-story level tests if you have a comprehensive suite of automated end-2-end regression tests. This may sound scary to some. However, it will become natural after you get used to it. After all, our goal is to release often, the best way to make it possible is to deploy more frequently and refine the process along the way.

 Deployed ClinicWise at a NY's McDonald's store.

During our family trip to the USA in 2013, I received a feature request from a ClinicWise customer one day. After putting the children sleep, I implemented the feature quickly, then triggered a run of the new and all regression tests in the CT Server overnight on my Laptop. I checked the build first thing in the morning: the new and all regression tests passed. However, I had issues with my 3G roaming device, unable to access the Internet to do a new deployment.

On the way to the Statue of Liberty, we stopped at a McDonald's for breakfast. While waiting for the children to finish the meal, I noticed the free WiFi was provided. I took out my MacBook from the backpack, connected to the free WiFi and pushed the new build to the production at the McDonald's.

Strictly speaking, I shouldn't be using a public network for work. My excuse was it can be done quickly. The confidence comes from I have been doing deployments numerous times, immediately after a green build on the CT server.

Developers stop and fix regression defects

"This (CI) is a difficult discipline, partly because developing a rapid build and test capability requires time, skill, and ongoing attention, and partly because stopping to fix problems can be distracting. But a great epiphany occurs once a software development team finds ways to do rapid builds and continuous integration and everyone faithfully stops to fix problems as soon as they are detected." - "Implementing Lean Software Development' book
[Poppendieck 06]

Most developers have never worked on projects with automated functional testing were properly implemented. They were not used to the quick feedback. Quite commonly, a developer was assigned a user story, he would estimate the effort it might take (typically 1 - 3 days) and worked on it. After he thinks it is done (usually manual testing by the developer), move on to the next user story. As you can see, during the sprint, this developer is not expecting much testing feedback from others.

The work pattern will change radically in DevOps (or real Agile). The testing feedback (mostly from automated regression tests) will be available continuously. As we know, a programmer's new check-in (for either implementing a new feature or a bug fix) to the code base often introduces new defects. If regression issues were detected quickly (maybe 15 minutes after the check-in) in a CT build, what will the team do? Frankly, most developers and managers don't not how, as this is new to them.

The simple and more effective answer is "Stop and fix regression defects". It is easier said than done. Kent Beck wrote this (*Toyota factory story*) in his classic "Extreme Programming Explained: Embrace Change" book in 1999, most will agree in principle. However, many are unwilling to do it properly.

- Manager: How does fix-regression time show up in my 'Burn Chart'?

- Developer: I am already in the middle of working on a new user story, I will fix all those regression defects towards the end of the sprint?

These thoughts are wrong. One of the most well-known software engineering rules is: fixing a bug earlier is not only much easier but also far cheaper.

Whole Team involved

Software development is a team activity. As we know, the best teamwork is only possible when everyone is actively involved with high moral. The whole team participates in activities with a strong focus on the end goal, and make concrete progress gradually. Mistakes or setbacks are unavoidable. But a good team detects early and is capable of making adjustments. In the context of software development, the most important activity is CT, which glues the whole team members together.

Here is an automated end-2-end user story test may be used in a sprint:

- Test engineers design and implement the test script

- Programmers don't usually get all things right on the first go. They can run this test script to help speed up refinement or debugging.

- Manual tester may utilise the scripts to speed up their exploratory testing

- Business Analyst may run the test script to verify against the requirement

- Business Analyst/Customer may utilise the script to get test data

- Business Analyst/Manager can use the script in Showcases

All user story tests together form the regression suite, which will be run in a CT server regularly.

- If a regression issue is detected, programmers can fix the newly introduced bug quickly.

- If all tests pass, deployment engineers may push the release to the production

The benefits will remain long after the product is delivered.

- Maintenance programmers can only rely on the regression test suite to make updates with confidence.

- The change manager may use the scripts to create product training videos.

The beauty of all the above is that all team members are involved. They don't need to spend time on unnecessary activities, such as

- Raise a defect on a defect tracking system

- Comment on the wordy and out-of-date (i.e. wrong) requirement on JIRA

- Find/update test data on a Confluence page

- ...

Once the lengthy manual testing phase is replaced with trusty test automation and a good CT process is in place, a software team becomes alive. The team members' focuses are on the software, their own software.

CT server is the heart of the team

"If I had to pick one reason our team has been so successful the past 7 years, our CI process is it. It's the pulse of our team, and if it stops, we all just about have a heart attack! When it's ticking along, we feel healthy and happy." - Lisa Crispin's blog post[2], 2010-08-23

---

[2]https://lisacrispin.com/2010/08/23/the-teams-pulse-cibuild-process/

Many 'Agile' teams manage software development based on JIRA, following a process learned from a 'SCRUM master' course. How ridiculous is that! The agile movements started around 1999. Two decades later, most software projects claimed "doing Agile" because they use JIRA or doing retrospectives. The foundation of Agile is test automation, only with that, the following activities make real sense.

- Code Refactoring

  Without automated unit tests, it is 'code changes' not 'code refactoring'

- Continuous Integration

  What's the value of CI if you don't run tests?

- Continuous Delivery

  Is CD really possible with 1+ month manual regression testing?

The bottom line is, without CT, How can you respond to customer changes quickly (the claimed main benefit of Agile over Waterfall)? The fact is that when the code base is complex, software engineers fear to make changes. All those burn up/down charts are velocity graph are just plain jokes. I am not saying the planning is not important, the planning shall be based on real stuff, not made-up story points. CT provides the reality, as Lisa Crispin said, it is the 'the pulse' of a software team.

Reward CT engineers well

"Test is harder than development. If you do good testing you need to put the best people in testing" - Gerald Weinberg, TestGuild Podcat #100[3]

I have worked in several different roles in my career, mostly as a software engineer and test automation/CT engineer. I agree with Gerald Weinberg, a true software legend, that coding is a much easier job compared to maintaining automated tests. Some people, especially developers, disagree. Well, I will tell you why.

---

[3]https://testguild.com/testing-harder-developing/

	Developers	CT Engineers
Work scope	Current user story	All user stories, from Sprint 1
Time to get work done	1 - 3 days	Minutes or hours
Pressure	If wrong, might be picked up in testing	The last defender of the quality
Dependencies	Few	Many, e.g. infrastructure, deployment, ...
Breadth of knowledge	Low - Medium	Medium - High, a good CT engineer shall have knowledge of each SDLC phase, as it can go wrong at any phase
Recognition	Medium - High	Low - Medium. Extreme High (as the best of the best) only in the world's top IT companies
Job satisfaction	Medium mostly	Stressful. Great only if all tests passed
Intensity of work	Low - Medium, take rest regularly	High
Financial	Medium	Low. Extreme High only in the world's top IT companies

Of course, here I refer to real CT engineers, who are very rare. If your company is lucky enough to have a few (who can create a few key test scripts and get them running in a CT server on the first day, and are capable to maintain all regression tests daily), please make sure to reward them well, not just financially. Let the whole company know that they are doing the most important work, and they are the best of the best.

Sadly, the work of CT engineers' is often not appreciated (at least not as deserved). One main reason is that the nature of CT engineers' work is **prevention**. The defects or issues were detected early by the CT process, and developers fixed them quickly. Unless the executives and managers monitor the daily builds in the CT servers, CT engineers' work is hardly visible. On the contrary, a manual tester who found a critical error in the production and the developer who fixed it will be cheered as 'Heroes'. This is very wrong! The work of CT engineers might have prevented hundreds of these kinds of bugs, just because the process was going well, people tend to take it for granted.

7. The Magic - Build Script

Now you have seen test executions in a BuildWise server, you might wonder:

1. How did the tests get invoked to run in BuildWise?

2. How can I customize the test executions such as excluding a specific test file?

3. How do I set one project to execute tests in parallel?

The answer: Build Scripts. In this chapter, I will show you how to use build scripts to customize your test executions.

7.1 What is Build Script?

A build task (also called build target) represents some piece of work that a build performs. This might be compiling some classes, creating a zip file, running tests, or publishing some archives to a repository.

Build tools

Language	Build tool	Default script file
C	Make	Makefile
Java	Ant	build.xml
Ruby	Rake	Rakefile
C#	MSBuild	.csproj (XML file)

Among all the build tools I have used over the last 20 years, I like Rake the best, for below simple and objective reasons:

1. Rakefile (the build file for Rake) is a **scripting language**

   Build scripts are better written in scripting languages, such as Ruby. As a comparison, XML (used by Ant and MSBuild) is not a scripting language.

2. Tasks in Rakefile are specified in **standard Ruby syntax**

   This means many benefits, we can

- use built-in Ruby functions directly in tasks, such as 'Net::SSH' and 'Net::SCP' modules to copy files to a remote machine

- use various libraries (called gems), such as 'Nokogiri' to parse XML documents

- define reusable functions to make the scripts easier to maintain

3. **Easy to learn**

   Also being a Ruby file, you can gain productivity on scripting Rakefiles with many tools that support Ruby:

   - programming editors or IDEs

   - syntax checking

   - pretty-print (reformat) the script

If your test scripts are in Ruby frameworks (such as popular RSpec), you will be very comfortable with using Rake in no time, as it is just another Ruby script with task definitions.

7.2 Use Build Script in BuildWise

Different from some other CI products, BuildWise is designed to give the users the maximum flexibility, yet simple to use. Instead of providing various user interfaces or modules for customizing test execution, BuildWise has only one generic and consistent way: using Rake build scripts.

Before I show setting up a build task in Buildwise, let's have a look at how it is done in a conventional CI server. For example, creating a SCP Task (*uploading files to a remote server*) in a popular CI product[1] requires filling a form like this:

---

[1]https://confluence.atlassian.com/bamboo/using-the-scp-task-in-bamboo-305759795.html

SCP Task configuration

Task description [   ]   ☑ Enable Task

Host * [   ]

Username * [   ]

Authentication Type * [Password   ▼]

Password * [   ]

Local Path * [   ]

Remote Path [   ]

▷ Advanced Options

I call this approach "make a simple task harder". Some may disagree: "*the above looks good and intuitive to me*". However, this thought is wrong for the CT professionals. Consider these requirements:

- only copy the files ending with ".zip"

- copy the files to a remote server and append the timestamp to the file name

Yes, the above via-UI approach might work with 'Advanced Options', or maybe not. This is just one of many drawbacks:

- **lack of flexibility**

  In reality, we will encounter scenarios that are more than basic usage.

- **lack of (or hard to do) version control**

  If I made a mistake, how can I revert to the last working version?

- **may have issues on upgrades**

  A task saved in the current version of CI server might not work the same way in the next upgrade, because the actual implementation of the task is totally unknown to you.

- **inefficient**

  Personally, I will get bored quite quickly if have to set up similar tasks this way multiple times.

- **inconsistencies**

  For a different CI product, the usage will be different. Even within the same CI server, inconsistencies (of UI) often exist for different features.

Classic scripting like the below addresses all the shortcomings above, and it is fun to work on. Your knowledge will grow with experience, and is not limited to a certain product that might not be around in a few years.

```ruby
# a standard way to copy files to remote servers in Ruby
require 'net/scp'
Net::SCP.upload!("remote.host.com", "username",  "/local/path", "/remote/path",
    :password => "password")
```

The reasons for big CI vendors' via-UI approach

The simple answer is to pursue maximum financial benefits. From a software vendor's view, the 'best way' to lock the customers in is to get them using technology in a proprietary way. Supporting an open standard will face fierce competition and smaller profit margins. For example, Selenium WebDriver is a W3C recommendation (i.e. standard), the only framework supported by all browser vendors, free, open-source, actively maintained and used by companies such as Facebook and Google. This seems a no-brainer for testing-tool vendors to dump their products and embrace Selenium WebDriver. However, the reality is not like this.

In April 2019, Microsoft deprecated its testing automation tool/framework Code UI and recommend Selenium WebDriver for testing web apps, which is applaudable. Still, Microsoft seems not to have plans to release a new testing tool for Selenium WebDriver. My explanation is that the projected return (revenues) on investment (efforts) might not be high enough to make it a business case. On the contrary, wrong but vendor-locking tools (such as Microsoft's Coded UI) usually make business sense to executives.

On the other hand, quite often, architects/managers who make purchase decisions lean towards the non-scripting approach, which has been proven wrong repeatedly for decades. This tendency is quite subtle, and it is hard to explain in words.

7.3 Configure Build Tasks in BuildWise

So far, our build project seems to just do one thing: running UI tests. It is configured in the project settings.

The build task `ci:ui_tests:quick` (you entered at project creation time) is under "Build Steps" section.

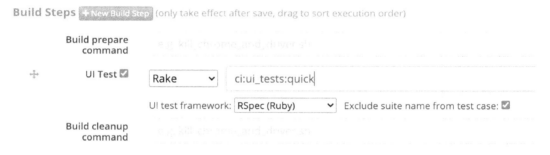

The `ci:ui_tests:quick` is defined in `Rakefile`.

7.4 Execute build tasks from the command line

You can verify a task by invoking it directly from the command. As a matter of fact, it is a best practice to do so: make sure it runs from the command line first before setting it in BuildWise.

```
> rake TASK_NAME
```

By default, Rake will use `Rakefile` in the current working directory. If the `Rakefile` is under a sub-directory, you can specify the path with `-f` flag.

```
> rake -f ui_tests/Rakefile TASK_NAME
```

7.5 Functional Testing (Sequential) Task

A task to run a set of test scripts one by one on the server machine (where the BuildWise server runs).

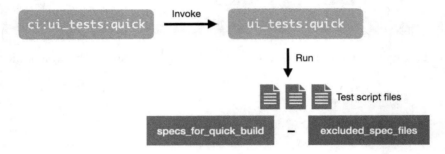

Let's look examine the `ui_tests:quick` task first. If you are not familiar with Rake or Ruby, don't worry, for most projects, the default task definitions will just work. Still, I recommend you studying the below to get a feel of it.

```
RSpec::Core::RakeTask.new("ui_tests:quick") do |t|
  specs_to_be_executed = buildwise_determine_specs_for_quick_build(
    specs_for_quick_build,  excluded_spec_files, $test_dir);
  buildwise_formatter = File.join(File.dirname(__FILE__), "buildwise_rspec_formatter.rb")
  t.rspec_opts = "--pattern my_own_custom_order --require #{buildwise_formatter}
                 #{specs_to_be_executed.join(' ')} --order defined"
end
```

You may invoke this task from the command line.

```
> cd agiletravel-ui-tests/selenium-webdriver-rspec
> rake ui_tests:quick
```

You shall see a few tests running in a Chrome browser.

 Try running the task from the command line first, before setting up the UI testing build step in a CT server.

The below are some functions and one variable used in the task definition:

- `buildwise_determine_specs_for_quick_build`

  A function determines the test scripts to be run. This function is defined in `build-wise.rake`, a generic helper which you just include and use it.

- `$test_dir`

  This global variable (defined in Rakefile) sets the absolute path of the test folder, where the test script files (e.g. foo_spec.rb) are located.

  ```
  $test_dir = File.expand_path( File.join( File.dirname(__FILE__), "spec" ) )
  ```

- `specs_for_quick_build`

  A function (in Rakefile) defines specific test script files that you want to include.

  ```
  def specs_for_quick_build
    [
      "01_login_spec.rb",
      "02_flight_spec.rb",
      "03_passenger_spec.rb",
      "04_payment_spec.rb",
    ]
  end
  ```

- `excluded_spec_files`

  A function (in Rakefile) defines specific test script files that you want to exclude.

  ```
  def excluded_spec_files
    ["debugging_spec.rb"]
  end
  ```

The `ci:ui_tests:quick` task simply invokes `ui_tests:quick` in a way that the results will be captured by the CT server.

```
desc "run quick tests from BuildWise"
task "ci:ui_tests:quick" => ["ci:setup:rspec"] do
  test_dir = File.expand_path(File.dirname(__FILE__))
  build_id = buildwise_start_build(:working_dir => test_dir)
  buildwise_run_sequential_build_target(build_id, "ui_tests:quick")
end
```

buildwise_start_build and buildwise_run_sequential_build_target are two helper functions defined in buildwise.rake.

You can verify this task, the same task that BuildWise server invokes, from the command line.

```
> rake -f selenium-webdriver-rspec/Rakefile ci:ui_tests:quick
```

You will find test results (in JUnit XML format) under spec/reports directory.

```
SPEC-Passenger.xml
SPEC-Payment.xml
SPEC-Select-Flights.xml
SPEC-User-Login.xml
```

7.6 Functional Testing (Parallel) Task

Different from sequential test execution, test scripts are executed in multiple build agents in the parallel mode.

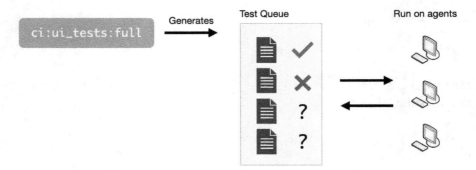

Hence, the task definition will be different. The main purpose of this task is to generate a list of test script files, which BuildWise will add them to a 'queue'.

```
desc "Running tests on build agents in parallel"
task "ci:ui_tests:full" => ["ci:setup:rspec"] do
  test_dir = File.expand_path(File.dirname(__FILE__))
  build_id = buildwise_start_build(:working_dir => test_dir,
                                   :ui_test_dir => ["spec"],
                                   :except => excluded_spec_files || [],
                                   :parallel => true
  )
  buildwise_montior_parallel_execution(build_id, :max_wait_time => 3600)
end
```

Below are some functions and one variable used in the task definition:

- `:parallel => true`

  Set the execution mode.

- `:ui_test_dir => ["spec"]`

  BuildWise assumes that all regression tests (in a specified directory: `ui_test_dir`) will be run in this mode. Exceptions can be specified in `excluded_spec_files` function (in the same `Rakefile`).

- `buildwise_montior_parallel_execution`

  A helper function defined in `buildwise.rake`.
  `max_wait_time` is the max time (in seconds) allowed for the build project. If exceeds that, a build will be considered 'failed'.

 Study the `Rakefile` in your test project, and try the followings:

- Invoke a build target from the command line

- Create a new build target to run certain tests

- Alter the test executions of your existing Sequential Build project:
  - Add one or more test scripts (*hint:* `spec_for_quick_build`)

  - Add all test scripts in a test folder

  - Exclude one or more test scripts (*hint:* `excluded_spec_files`)

  - Change to run the newly created build target

8. Manage a project

In this chapter, I will demonstrate how to manage a build project in a CT server. While the instructions (and screenshots) are specific to BuildWise, the rationale of each CT feature applies to other CT servers.

8.1 Build Step Management

A build (a run of functional tests) consists of one or multiple build steps.

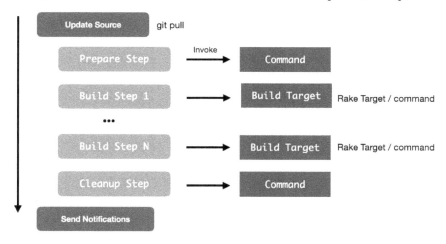

A build step in BuildWise simply invokes a Rake build target or a command. If the return value of a build step proceess is not 0 (i.e. successful), this build step is considered failed, and the whole build ends.

Add a new build step

Enter the name of the new step, then set the build target.

Change the order of build steps

To change the execution order of the steps, simply drag to re-arrange.

Disable/Delete a build step

You may disable a build step by unchecking the checkbox next to the step name.

To delete a disabled build step permanently, click the trash icon on the right.

8.2 Common Pre-Functional-Testing Tasks

While the main build task for a CT process is to run automated functional tests, we can add some other build tasks to assist the test execution. These tasks may be set in two ways: Build prepare command or a build step, as shown below:

Reset data

Test data is a part of testing, and test automation has high requirements on test data. A good test automation practice is to reset the test data to a known state.

Clear test emails on a fake email test server: MailCatcher (*using Selenium WebDriver*).

```
desc "Clear emails in Mailcatcher"
task "emails:clear" do
  driver = Selenium::WebDriver.for(:chrome)
  driver.get("http://mail.server:1080") # mail catcher web interface
  sleep 1
  driver.execute_script "window.confirm = function() { return true; }"
  driver.execute_script "window.alert = function() { return true; }"
  river.execute_script "window.prompt = function() { return true; }"
  driver.find_element(:link_text, "Clear").click
  sleep 1
  driver.quit
end
```

Clear files generated:

```
desc "Clear the files under download directory"
task "downloads:clear" do
  # clear PDF and Excel
end
```

Test Scripts Stats

In the same project as above, I included a reusable task to extract stats of test scripts:

- the number of test cases

- the number of page classes

- the number of functions in page classes

- the number of test steps in test cases, page classes and the test helpers

```ruby
desc "Generate stats for UI tests"
task "test:stats" do
  # ...
end
```

Here is a sample output for one of my own projects: ClinicWise.

Build #5210	clinicwise-full-build/sources zhimin$ rake -f ui-tests/Rakefile test:stats

```
clinicwise-full-build/sources zhimin$ rake -f ui-tests/Rakefile test:stats
+------------+---------+---------+---------+--------+
| TEST       | LINES   | SUITES  | CASES   | LOC    |
|            | 27506   | 260     | 612     | 21307  |
+------------+---------+---------+---------+--------+
| PAGE       | LINES   | CLASSES | METHODS | LOC    |
|            | 11695   | 260     | 2065    | 8705   |
+------------+---------+---------+---------+--------+
| HELPER     | LINES   | COUNT   | METHODS | LOC    |
|            | 455     | 1       | 44      | 343    |
+------------+---------+---------+---------+--------+
| TOTAL      | 39656   |         |         | 30355  |
+------------+---------+---------+---------+--------+
```

Build #5210

❯ **Prepare Build**

Git Pull ✔

Prepare ✔

❯ **Build Steps**

Test Stats ✔

Deploy ✔

LOC means 'Line of Code', in this context, code means 'test scripts'.

Common CI tasks

BuildWise can be configured to run common CI tasks as well, such as:

- Unit Testing

- Code Coverage

- Deployment

I did have some of these build steps for my web apps. However, I prefer separating CT from CI these days. That is, I do build, unit testing and deployment in a CI server, such as Jenkins. Then execute functional tests in a CT server, such as BuildWise.

BuildWise can be configured as a CI server, but I don't recommend it. For most of the projects that I was involved in, there were some forms of CI (some even tried to run UI tests, but all failed), but very few of them are real CT. For this reason, I decide not to show the CI task examples in BuildWise in order to stay on the main track and avoid distractions.

Warm-up Test Servers

After a new build is deployed on a test server, it usually requires a restart. This might take some time. If we run functional tests immediately after, it will be a good idea to warm up the servers:

```ruby
desc "Warm up a set of test servers"
task "warm_up_servers" do
  warm_up_start_time = Time.now
  warm_up_threads = []
  ["1", "2", "3", "4", "5". "6"].each do |sid|
    warm_up_threads << warm_up_server(sid)
  end
  warm_up_threads.each do |t|
    t.join
  end
  puts "[INFO] Warm up time: #{Time.now - warm_up_start_time}"
end


def warm_up_server(sid)
    require 'nokogiri'
    require 'open-uri'
    Thread.new do
      sleep 0.1 # wait a bit
      url = "https://ci#{sid}.test.server" # test server url
      puts "Warm up #{url}"
      doc = Nokogiri::HTML(open(url,  :ssl_verify_mode => OpenSSL::SSL::VERIFY_NONE))
      #  puts document.css("#page_content").inner_text.strip
    end
end
```

8.3 Clone an existing project

Objective

To set up another build configuration with the same test script repository.

Action

The easiest way to create a similar project is to clone an existing one.

1. Open an existing project's setting page

   Edit project: AgileTravel Quick Build RSpec (agiletravel-quick-build-rspec) [Duplicate]

2. Click '**Duplicate**' button.

   Duplicate project: AgileTravel Quick Build RSpec

   Quickly clone an existing build project, you may customize the setting later.

New Project Name:	AgileTravel Quick Build RSpec
New Project Identifier:	
Execution Mode:	◉ **Sequential** ○ **Parallel**
UI Test Task:	-f selenium-webdriver-rspec/Rakefile ci:ui_tests:quick
Branch:	default to master

   [Clone] [Cancel]

   Update the following three fields:

   - Name
   - Identifier, it must be unique.
   - UI Test Task, use another task name defined in your *Rakefile*.

   Click "**Clone**" button.

For parallel testing, which we will cover later, we need to set a couple of more fields.

New Project Name:	AgileTravel Parallel Build RSpec
New Project Identifier:	agiletravel-parallel-build-rspec
Execution Mode:	○ **Sequential** · **Parallel**
App name		

The name of application to be tested, the Application setting in BuildWise Agent shall match this.

Work directory on Agents:

The checked out or cloned top directory from repository, e.g. /Users/me/myproject

UI Test Task: -f selenium-webdriver-rspec/Rakefile ci:ui_tests:full

8.4 Build Artifacts

Objective

Build artifacts are the outputs of the build process. You want to keep them available after a build is completed.

Action

Specify the files you want to save in the project's artifacts settings. The paths are relative to the checked-out project path. Wildcards such as `*.zip` may be used.

Files/Directories to archive (relative to the project root dir, separate by ';')

recipes/tmp/invoices.xls;recipes/tmp/*.zip

Here is a sample build with artifacts.

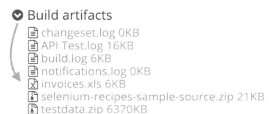

❷ Build artifacts
  📄 changeset.log 0KB
  📄 API Test.log 16KB
  📄 build.log 6KB
  📄 notifications.log 0KB
  📄 invoices.xls 6KB
  📄 selenium-recipes-sample-source.zip 21KB
  📄 testdata.zip 6370KB

8.5 Enable the project's API key

Objective

To allow the external programs to manage the build projects in BuildWise.

Action

Enable the API key for a build project.

For example, making an HTTP post request to `/api/projects/PROJECT_ID/trigger_-build?api_key=API_KEY` will trigger a new build on the BuildWise server.

8.6 Notifications

Objective

Send notifications of the build outcome to the team. The configured notifications (can be several of them) will be sent automatically at the end of a build, by the BuildWise server.

Configurations

BuildWise supports the following notification mechanism:

- Slack

  A convenient way to send notifications to all the team members.

Sample notifications.

- Email

  An old-fashioned yet practical notification mechanism.

- Wemo Smart Wi-Fi Plugs

  Send signals to a pair of smart power plugs to turn on/off powered Wi-Fi devices that are identified by IP address. Whenever possible, I like to implement build lava lamps with this notification mechanism.

	Active?	○ Yes ● No	
Wemo Location (IP) when failed		10.0.0.12	Check status
Wemo Location (IP) when successful		10.0.0.11	Check status

- TP-Link Smart Wi-Fi Plugs

  Similar to Wemo. TP-Link notifications can be extended to the plugs on the Internet (not limited to the LAN).

	Active?	○ Yes ● No	
Plug device name when failed		TP-Link 02 Red	Check status
Plug device name when successful		TP-Link 01 Green	Check status

- HTTP Callback

  Make an HTTP post request to the configured URL (also known as webhook), with the build status in the request body.

	Active?	○ Yes ● No	Send test notification
Webhook URL		e.g. https://your_ci.server/...	

BuildWise server is open-sourced. It is quite convenient to extend to support a new notification mechanism such as Microsoft Teams.

8.7 Project Statistics

- Build result and time

  The below chart shows the results and duration of the builds (for TestWise Desktop app) in the current quarter.

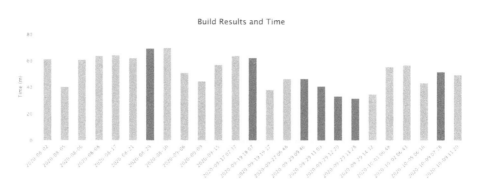

- Test case count

  The below chart shows the number of UI test cases over the last 31 months for WhenWise web app.

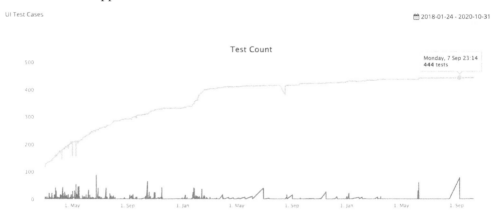

- Total executions (count and pass rate)

  The below chart shows the total number of test executions and the overall pass rates over the last 7 years for ClinicWise web app.

	Selected date range	All
Builds:	23	2031
Total test case executions:	13,979	615,883
Total execution time:	3 days 19 hours	145 days 1 hour
Pass rate:	99.8%	97.9%
Date range:	2020-01-01 to 2020-09-26 *(268 days 21 hours)*	2013-03-31 to 2020-09-26 *(7 years 180 days)*

8.8 Hide a project

For a build project you want to hide, navigate to **Preferences** (click *admin* dropdown and select *preferences*), then toggle a project to show status there.

You may permanently delete a hidden project.

 Try to practice the above in your BuildWise server.

9. Manage builds

In previous chapters, we have covered the basic operations with a build (running a set of functional testers) in a CT server.

- View Change Log

- Trigger a build manually

- Cancel an in-progress build

In this chapter, I will explore other operations that we can commonly do with a build.

9.1 Trigger a build via API

Objective

Trigger a build by a program.

Prerequisite

The API key of the project, which serves as the authentication token, has been set.

Project API Key	cvCiWpv8fJDzQHRIqPNE
Generate Disable	POST to /api/projects/agiletravel-quick-build-rspec/trigger_build?api_key=API_KEY.

Action

Send an HTTP post message with the project API key to the CT server.

A build trigged by API can be identified by the text at the end of the build page.

⊙ *triggered by* API at 2020-10-21 08:50:55

Curl from the command line

The easiest way to trigger a BuildWise build is to run a Curl command from the command line.

```
curl -d "" -X POST http://localhost/api/projects/agiletravel-quick-build-rspec/trigger_bu\
ild?api_key=cvCiWpv8fJDzQHRIqPNE
```

If successful, the output will be as below:

```
{"status":"OK","build_id":3}
```

Ruby script

```
require 'net/http'
require 'uri'
url = "http://localhost/api/projects/1/trigger_build?api_key=cvCiWpv8fJDzQHRIqPNE"
result = Net::HTTP.post URI(url), ""
puts result
```

GUI tools such as Postman

I prefer the 'Manual' way to trigger a build for functional testing

I recommend using the 'Manual' way for builds that run automated functional tests. The reason is simple: a successful test execution of UI tests relies on many factors:

- the target server and client machines are ready (ie. not performing a software update or virus check),

- the dependent supporting services such as fake SMTP servers are working,

- network and hardware conditions,

- test data, ..., etc.

In other words, executing automated UI testing takes a long time (unless you have dedicated test labs with thousands of machines, like Facebook and Google),

Build via scheduling and repository hooks might sound cool. However, they are complex. Therefore, it can easily cause failed builds with many false alarms. Generally speaking, they are more suitable for the builds with unit testing only (good unit tests isolated dependencies).

For my own projects, I only trigger the build the Manual way.

9.2 Schedule a build

Objective

Schedule builds to run automatically at a specific time or periodically.

Scheduled build on macOS/Linux

Firstly, create a shell script to trigger a project build with the API key.

```
#!/bin/sh
curl -d "" -X POST http://localhost/api/projects/9/trigger_build?api_key=SECRET
```

Verify the shell script. Then set up a cron job to schedule a run of this script. Run `crontab -e` in a terminal and set a cron job in an editor (default to Vi).

```
50 19 * * 1-5 cd ~/bin && ./trigger_buildwise_build.sh
```

The above example will trigger a build 19:50 on every weekday, just like this one.

AgileTravel Quick Build RSpec 📈
2020-10-22 19:50:00
4a3f56cf.1: OK ⏱ 40 sec

Scheduled build on Windows

Use Windows built-in 'Task Scheduler'.

9.3 Add Build Summary

Objective

Add summarised information to a build, to let the team know about a particular build.

Action

☐ Add summary

Enter the text in the popup dialog.

Change the build's summary   ✕

| Server rebooted during build, ignore. |

Cancel   OK

The summary text is shown on the build.

You can click the summary text to edit.

9.4 Invalidate a build

Objective

To mark a build invalid, so that it will not be included in the reports.

Action

On the build page, click the action drop-down and select '**Invalidate**'.

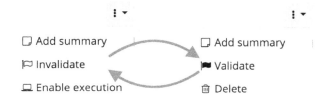

You can revert this operation to mark an invalid build to valid.

9.5 Delete a build

Objective

To permanently delete a build.

Action

You can only delete the builds that have been marked as **Invalid**.

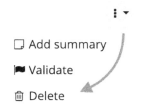

9.6 View and download build artifacts

Build artifacts will be shown on the build page after a build is completed.

There are two types: log files generated by the CT server, and specified files (as configured in the project setting).

The files are stored within a sub-directory under the CT server's working folder, such as `.buildwise/work/api-testing-recipes-ruby/artifacts/05880-20201023085740`.

 Be aware of large artifacts, which may take lots of disk space over time.

9.7 View build logs

Build logs can help to debug the build errors which commonly include:

- Build configuration errors, e.g. unable to locate a file or directory.

- A library (used in test scripts) was not found on the machine

- Failed to load test script due to a syntax error

In BuildWise, the build logs are automatically archived as the build artifacts of a build.

Build Log

The log for the overall build process. If a build ends immediately, check out this log.

```
Build #5880            ● UI Test Results ( 67 tests )
                       ● Build log
  ✓ Build Prepare        2020-10-23 08:57:39 +1000 [Build] Start
                         2020-10-23 08:57:39 +1000 [INFO] buildwise-build.rb production | finding a build |5880
```

Step Log

The log for a specific build step.

∨ Build Steps

☆ API Test   ✕

∨ Finalize Build

```
Failure/Error: return gem_original_require(path)

LoadError:
  cannot load such file -- faker
# ./recipes/test_helper.rb:5:in `<top (required)>'
# ./recipes/spec/ch02_soap_spec.rb:1:in `load'
```

 Try to practice the above for your build project in BuildWise.

10. Sequential E2E Test Execution

In Chapter 2, we set up a build project quickly in BuildWise to run UI tests. Now with a better understanding of CT and how test execution is configured in BuildWise, let's explore the execution of automated UI tests in CT further. After all, it is the core of CT.

10.1 Sequential Mode

So far, our automated tests have been executed on the BuildWise server machine. I call it "Sequential Mode", as opposed to "Parallel Mode" (ie. tests are run in multiple machines. We will cover this important topic in late chapters). I recommend starting CT with Sequential Mode, as it is more manageable and many engineers would find similarities from their past experience with the traditional CI servers.

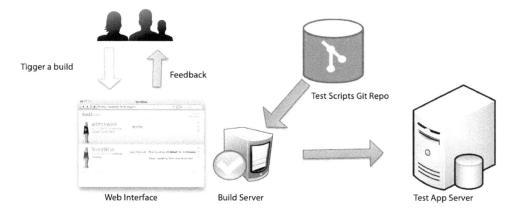

10.2 Pre-requisite

Test scripts can be run from the command line on the build server, with the below software installed:

- Browser, e.g. Chrome

- WebDriver for Browser, e.g. ChromeDriver

- Script language and its libraries, e.g. Ruby and RSpec

For example, the below command runs a RSpec test:

```
> rspec spec/login_spec.rb
```

10.3 Decide what tests to be included

The very first question to the engineer who is planning the test execution in CT is: *"what tests do we run?"* A vague answer "every test" is not practical, moreover, it is mostly impossible to execute all tests one by one in Sequential mode. Due to the nature of UI test automation (brittle, especially for dynamic web apps), the chance of getting a green build with a large test suite is very slim without auto-retry in Parallel mode (we will cover that in a later chapter).

 Factors that affect UI test execution stability:

- Stability and Performance of the target server

- Performance of the machine runs the tests

- Network

- Quality of the test scripts

For example, the regression test suite of WhenWise App has 444 user-story-level selenium tests, with around 24,000 test steps. No matter how good the test scripts are, it is very unlikely that all 24,000 test steps will pass over 4 hours' test execution in a browser.

This does not mean there isn't any value in executing automated functional tests in Sequential mode, far from that. We need to be practical and selective. We will run all tests in Parallel mode. But in sequential mode, we run a small set of key tests to cover the core business functions (80/20 rule).

Why not just go for Parallel mode completely?

Some may wonder why bother running a subset in sequential mode, why not just run all tests in parallel mode? The reasons are:

1. Parallel Testing requires more infrastructure

   In many organisations, it usually takes weeks (or months) to get the infrastructure you needed to set up a proper parallel testing lab.

2. Test Scripts might need to be rewritten to support parallel execution

   In Sequential mode, tests are executed one by one exclusively by 'one user'. In Parallel mode, we need to make sure all test executions are independent of each other.

3. Sequential Build might be useful for non-regression uses

   Other team members such as business analysts may find test automation scripts helpful in creating application data.

10.4 Select test script files in the build script

Once we decide on the What, the next step is How, which is set in the build script (Rakefile). I covered this in Chapter 7. Just a quick recap here.

Specific test scripts

```
# list test files to be run in a sequential build
def specs_for_quick_build
  [
    "01_login_spec.rb",
    "02_flight_spec.rb",
    "03_passenger_spec.rb",
    "04_payment_spec.rb",
    "not_exists_spec.rb" # not found ones will be excluded anyway
  ]
end
```

All test scripts in a folder

```
# all test scripts files in a folder
def specs_for_quick_build
  # $test_dir is defined earlier: the folder contains UI tests
  Dir.glob("#{$test_dir}/*_spec.rb").collect{|x| File.basename(x) }
end
```

Exclude certain tests

```
def excluded_spec_files
  ["debugging_spec.rb", "unstable_spec.rb"]
end
```

10.5 Define a build target

Define a build target that you can invoke to run the selected tests from the command line. Below is a sample sequential build target (mostly reusable) for BuildWise, which I have covered in Chapter 7.

```
task "ci:ui_tests:quick" => ["ci:setup:rspec"] do
  test_dir = File.expand_path(File.dirname(__FILE__))
  build_id = buildwise_start_build(:working_dir => test_dir)
  buildwise_run_sequential_build_target(build_id, "ui_tests:quick")
end

RSpec::Core::RakeTask.new("ui_tests:quick") do |t|
  specs_to_be_executed = buildwise_determine_specs_for_quick_build(
    specs_for_quick_build,  excluded_spec_files, $test_dir);
  buildwise_formatter = File.join(File.dirname(__FILE__), "buildwise_rspec_formatter.rb")
  t.rspec_opts = "--pattern my_own_custom_order --require #{buildwise_formatter}
                 #{specs_to_be_executed.join(' ')} --order defined"
end
```

Verify build target from the command line

It is a good practice to verify the build target from the command line before using it in a CT project configuration.

```
> cd agiletravel-ui-tests/selenium-webdriver-rspec
> rake ci:ui_tests:quick
```

The test results are not important at this stage. Just make sure the correct set of tests are run.

10.6 Task Configuration in BuildWise

The core task of CT is to run automated functional tests, as in the sample one below.

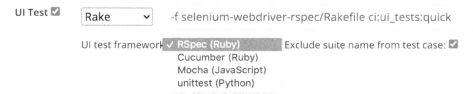

You may customize the build project with more build tasks.

Prepare task

There are a set of operations you may want to do before running the test suite, such as clearing emails in the test mail server and closing all browsers. This is called 'prepare task' in BuildWise. To enable one, specify the path to a batch command (or shell script in Unix/macOS).

Build prepare   /Users/zhimin/bin/clear_mails_in_mailcatcher.sh
command

Manage build tasks

A build task in BuildWise is simply invoking a build target in a Rakefile. Besides the main 'UI testing' task, you may add more build tasks such as "deployment" and "test stats".

Build Steps ➕ New Build Step (only take effect after save, drag to sort execution order)

Drag and drop build tasks to set the execution order.

Cleanup task

The 'cleanup task' is a command that runs after all the build tasks are completed.

Build cleanup command   e.g. delete_docker_agents.sh

10.7 Test Execution Order

Typically, the test scripts are executed in either alphabetical or specified order. If the test executions are invoked via a build script such as Rake, you have the flexibility to set the execution order.

10.8 Feedback during the build

On Sequential mode, BuildWise starts a process to execute a set of automated tests. Naturally, we want to get feedback as early as possible, that is, after the execution of a test script is finished (while the build is still in progress), its test results will be shown on the CT server (web interface). The engineers can act on the feedback immediately.

10.9 Analyse test reports

The test results of automated test execution in CI/CT servers are in JUnit reports (in XML), CI/CT servers represent them in a more user-friendly format via a web page. From test reports (with history), we can gain many insights such as:

- Failed tests in this build

- When was the last successful run of one test?

- Overall execution reliability of one test script

- Big changes for execution time for a specific test

- ...

10.10 Anti-Pattern: Split tests into multiple sub-builds

In the next chapter, I will show the best practices for sequential builds in CT. Here, I will highlight one common mistake for running tests sequentially in CI/CT. The mistake is so common that I have seen this in every Jenkins project for executing UI tests. They all failed badly. The mistake is breaking a test suite into multiple sub-sequential-build projects. Often these sub-build projects are named: suite 1, suite 2, ..., etc.

In my opinion, the root cause of splitting tests is that the CT engineers did CT with unit-testing mindset. At first, setting up the execution of a few simple UI tests in CI/CT is not hard. Some engineers who don't have real CT experience thought running UI tests is not much different from unit tests. Gradually, problems start to emerge:

- Long execution time

  The build time grows quickly with more functional tests added in, 30 mins, 1 hour, ..., etc. Due to the lack of quick feedback, the team gradually lost interests in the CT process.

- High failure rate

  It was getting harder to get a green build, and quickly became impossible.

It is quite natural (in a bad way) for CT engineers to break the test scripts into smaller suites.

Why it is bad?

- Confusion

  If a task (needing to be done regularly) is split into 8 subtasks and the success of the task depends on the success of all the subtasks. This surely requires some management effort. Please note, the divide-and-conquer strategy (which is good for solving a new and complex problem) does not apply here.

  It is not hard to imagine that someone later would say "6 out 8 suites passed, the test failures in the rest 2 might be a test data issue. I think overall this build is OK. I will get manual testers to verify, ...". This is when the team starts to lose trust in the CT process.

- Test prioritization

  It is easier to lead to 'prioritizing test'. For example, Suite 1 - 3 are must-pass tests, Suite 7 - 9 are low priority ones. What will happen after a few weeks? The engineers will naturally ignore test failures beyond Suite 1-3. Very soon, Suite 4 - 9 don't get run often and quickly outdated. This mindset will soon lead to Suite 1 is a must-pass, Suite 3 is alow priority, ... etc.

Ironically, for nearly every failed CT project I have seen, functional testing was 100% performed by manual testers, however, the so-called 'CI/CD' build process was still scheduled to run daily. The team simply did not care it anymore.

What is the solution?

You shall NOT run all tests in a sequential build, splitting them makes it worse. The solution is to run ALL tests in a parallel mode, which I will cover in later chapters.

The more intriguing question for this common mistake is beyond the technical aspect. Given functional testing in CT is pretty much universally applicable, why do so many CT (often called DevOps) engineers were allowed to repeat the same and obvious mistakes?

 I usually set up a sequential build (for selected tests) and a parallel build (for all tests) on the first day for clients.

I think it is a failure of leadership. Executives don't understand CT, but like the idea of CT. So some fake engineers who don't have the skills were put in the position. I did meet a few DevOps engineers who really want to learn but had no access to mentoring.

11. Sequential Test Execution Best Practices

As you may already know, it is easy to make mistakes in CT. In this chapter, I will share some of the best practices that I have learned from over 14 years of experience in hands-on CT.

11.1 Limit the test count

We simply cannot run many automated UI tests in the sequential mode, for the reasons of reliability and long execution time. In other words, to get a high-chance of green build with quick feedback, there is a cap on the number of tests you can put in a sequential build. Some may say: "there is little value doing sequential builds then". From the perspective of regression testing, yes, you shall go for parallel builds.

Still, there are benefits with sequential builds:

1. Start with a Sequential build, and move to Parallel later

    Setting up a parallel build is more complex and requires more infrastructure. By starting with a sequential build, which is fine for a small set of test scripts. You will gain a lot of experience with UI test execution, and it will be easier to switch to a parallel build when necessary.

2. Test executions other than the purpose of regression testing

    In terms of the value, regression testing tops the benefits of CT. There are still other benefits with automated end-2-end test executions, such as smoke testing, cross-browser testing, showcase demos and test data creation (for business analysts and customers). Sequential builds are very suitable for the above.

11.2 Show test results immediately

Feedback is important on test execution. After I trigger a build, my immediate desire is to know whether the failed tests of the last build pass or not. If not, I can work on it (on my local machine) while the build is still in progress.

Ideally, when the execution of a test script (please note, not a test case. One test script file may contain multiple test cases) is finished, the test result will be shown on the CT server's build page.

11.3 Capture the error stack trace

When a test failure/error is detected in CT, a CT engineer's immediate reactions are **Why** and **Where**.

The answers for the above example are:

- **Why?**

  Assertion failure. Test scripts expected "Wendy Tester" but got "Bob Tester" on the app.

- **Where?**

  Line 43 at `spec/03_passenger_spec.rb`.

Together with the captured screenshot (see below), an experienced test automation engineer shall have a good idea of the cause for the test failure, in seconds.

11.4 Capture the error screenshot

A screenshot of the application when the test failure/error occurred will help engineers to identify the cause quickly.

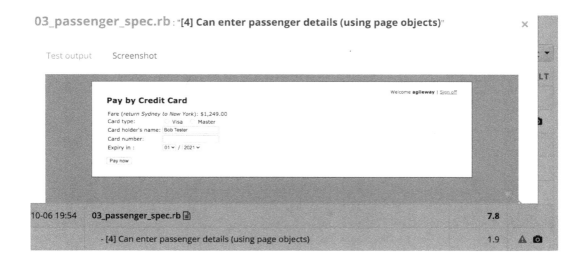

Capturing test executions into videos (or screenshots for every test step) might sound cool. However, it is often counter-productive in reality. One screenshot of the application when the failure occurred is good enough. For further investigation, it is far easier (and better) to just rerun the test on your machine instead of downloading and watching the video. I have seen a few projects encountered CT server crashes due to 'run of disk space errors' with the purchased 'video capture' option.

11.5 View test script content

CT is a team activity. If test scripts are written well, all team members (including business analysts) shall understand them. However, often not all the team members have easy access to the test scripts for various reasons, such as no testing tool licenses. By showing test scripts on the CT server, the team members may view and review the test script directly in their browsers.

01_login_spec.rb	×	TIME (S)

```
28    it "[1] Can sign in OK" do
29      goto_page("/login")
30      driver.find_element(:id, "username").send_keys("agileway")
31      driver.find_element(:id, "password").send_keys("testwise")
32      driver.find_element(:name, "commit").click
33      # selenium does not have browser.text yet
34      try_for(3) {  expect(driver.page_source).to include("Welcome")}
35      driver.find_element(:link_text, "Sign off").click
36      puts "[stdout] Signed out"
37    end
38
39    it "[1] User failed to sign in due to invalid password", :tag => "showcase" do
40      goto_page("/login")
41      login_page = LoginPage.new(driver)
42      login_page.login("agileway", "badpass")
43      expect(driver.page_source).to include("Invalid email or password")
44    end
```

	TIME (S)
(line 28)	14.9
(line 31)	10.6
(line 34)	7.1
(line 36)	1.9
(line 39)	8.9
(line 42)	2.3
(line 44)	2.1
07-26 21:14 01_login_spec.rb 🗎 Output	6.7
- [1] Can sign in OK	1.9
- [1] User failed to sign in due to invalid password	0.9

This small feature is great to get the team involved in CT, with ongoing benefits such as:

- Find out test data, "*what's the test admin user?*"

- Review test script, "*the assertion on line 19 seems incorrect*"

11.6 View test output

Showing the output of test executions on CT can be quite helpful. For example, the test step below prints out 'the booking number returned from the app'.

```
puts("booking number: " + driver.find_element(:id, 'booking_number').text)
```

Its output is shown on a BuidlWise CT build.

07-26 21:15 04_payment_spec.rb 🗎 Output	14.9	
booking number: 12239		
- [5] Book flight with payment	10.6	OK

The benefits of capturing the test output:

- Test Data (for the team)

  The data from test executions is helpful for quickly getting to a specific scenario (e.g. *a job application number*) in the app. Here are some sample uses:
    - a manual tester helps to verify a test failure
    - a business analyst finds the test data for a certain scenario

- Debugging test scripts

  The output can assist engineers in debugging test scripts when errors/failures occurred.

11.7 Customize test executions with Environment Variables

When running a functional test against a different environment, we often need to change to a different server URL or test user logins. It is a bad practice to change the test script back and forth. Creating a new Git branch is even worse. A simple approach is to let test scripts use the environment variables.

In the BuildWise project setting, you can set environment variables there, which will be passed to the test execution.

Server

Quite often, we want to run the same test suite against different server environments such as DEV and TEST servers. It is a bad practice to hard-code app server URL in the test scripts. Instead of hard coding the URL in a test script,

```
driver.get("http://whenwise.agileway.net")
```

we use the one set in the environment variable BASE_URL.

```
driver.get(ENV["BASE_URL"] || "https://whenwise.agileway.net")
```

The || operator here means: use the supplied one (`https://whenwise.agileway.net`) if the `BASE_URL` environment variable is not set.

Browser

Just like the target server URL, it is a good practice to use an environment variable for the browser type as well. Don't hard code

```
driver = Selenium::WebDriver.for(:chrome)
```

do this instead.

```
env_browser = ENV["BROWSER"]
driver = Selenium::WebDriver.for(env_browser ? env_browser.downcase.to_sym : :chrome)
```

BuildWise server provides a convenient interface (radio buttons) to set this special `BROWSER` environment variable.

Headless mode

Headless testing is running a browser test without showing the browser UI. In the Agile-Travel sample test scripts, the `test_helper` uses an environment variable `BROWSER_HEAD-LESS` to control whether headless or not.

```
if $TESTWISE_BROWSER_HEADLESS || ENV["BROWSER_HEADLESS"] == "true"
  the_chrome_options.add_argument("--headless")
end
```

To enable executing tests in headless mode in BuildWise, simply add an environment variable `BROWSER_HEADLESS` with the value `true` in the project setting.

11.8 Clone build project for different purposes

Quite often, we want to run a different set of automated tests (with the same Git repository) for different purposes, such as

- Smoke tests on System Test

- Key tests on Dev

- User stories in Sprint X

- Key tests on Edge browser

- Test data for business analysts

- ...

Though setting up a new project in BuildWise is not hard, as you have seen in early chapters, still, it is easier to clone an existing one.

1. Go to an existing project, click the 'Duplicate' button

Edit project: BuildWise Sequential (buildwise-sequential)

2. Specify a new project name and the main UI testing task

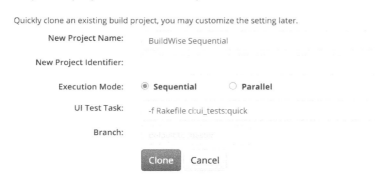

You can customize the build project settings later.

11.9 Dynamic Ordering

Usually, test scripts are executed in alphabetical order. This is not optimal. Assuming Test #99 (out of 100) failed in a recent build. As a test automation engineer, I would act quickly and fix it (verified locally). Then I will trigger another run in CT. Then I have to wait got a long time to find out whether Test #99 passes or not in CT. That's frustrating, isn't it?

Let me show you a better way in BuildWise with two sample builds below:

First run

On the first run, the 3rd test `03_passenger_spec` failed.

⊙ ▲	TEST FILE (6 test cases in 4 test scripts files)	TIME (S)	RESULT
10-16 17:57	**01_login_spec.rb** 📄 Output	**9.0**	OK
10-16 17:57	**02_flight_spec.rb** 📄	**9.9**	OK
10-16 17:57	**03_passenger_spec.rb** 📄	**8.3**	Failed
10-16 17:57	**04_payment_spec.rb** 📄 Output	**8.4**	OK

Second run

On the next run, the first executed test is `03_passenger_spec`.

⊙ ▲	TEST FILE (6 test cases in 4 test scripts files)	TIME (S)	RESULT
10-16 17:58	**03_passenger_spec.rb** 📄	**7.2**	Failed
10-16 17:58	**04_payment_spec.rb** 📄 Output	**12.0**	OK
10-16 17:58	**02_flight_spec.rb** 📄	**9.4**	OK
10-16 17:58	**01_login_spec.rb** 📄 Output	**7.2**	OK

How come? This is because I turned on 'Dynamic Ordering' setting for this project in BuildWise.

Sequential Test Execution (Run test sequentially on BuildWise server)

Intelligent Ordering   On

Setting the execution order of test scripts by the past execution history.

BuildWise will analyse the recent execution results of each test script, and rearrange the execution order 'intelligently', Basically, the recently added and frequently failed test scripts will be given priority to run first.

12. Parallel Test Execution

A good CT process provides quick feedback to developers, ideally minutes after check-ins. However, the nature of test execution via GUI is slow (comparing to unit testing). The only practical solution is parallel test execution, that is, distributing test scripts to multiple build machines (often called build agents or slaves) to run them in parallel. In this chapter, I will show parallel test execution in a CT server.

12.1 Build Agents

Build Agents participate in a CT build to execute automated tests. In the context of testing web apps, a build agent invokes test scripts to drive a browser window to verify the app.

During a parallel build, a build agent performs the following steps repeatedly:

1. Check the server (with configured polling interval) whether there is an active build. If yes, continue to

2. Get one test script from the server

3. Run the test script

4. Return the test results to the server

5. Go to step 2 until the build completes

Build Agent Machines

The requirement for a build agent machine is simple: like an end-user computer. Build agent machines can be physical or virtual machines, as long as they can communicate to the BuildWise server and the target websites.

- Virtual Machines (VM)

    A virtual machine is an emulation of a computer system using virtualization software such as VMware and VirtualBox. The main advantages of VM are low cost and easy to replicate. Commonly, the virtualization infrastructure has already been used in some medium/large companies.

Setting up your own VMs is quite easy. Install VirtualBox (free) and import a free 90-day OS image from Microsoft[1].

> I recommend starting with VMs on a local computer, as it can be set up quickly without dependencies. A laptop computer with 16GB RAM shall be enough to host 3 VMs.

- Cloud-based VM instances

  As we know, the trend these days is to 'move infrastructure to cloud'. Certainly, build agents are suitable (even more than the servers, in my opinion) to be hosted on cloud platforms such as AWS, Azure and Vultr. The hardware requirement for a build agent machine is generally low. A typical cloud-based Linux VM costs between $20-$40 per month.

  > Cloud-based VM is the best for medium/large companies if done by competent infrastructure engineers. Over the years, I have seen too many resume-driven infrastructure engineers (sometimes called DevOps engineers) over-complicated cloud deployments, and resulted in the very unreliable infrastructure (*and often took a long time*).
  >
  > The setup of build agent machines shall be easy and straightforward: just a standard user desktop machine. If the infrastructure is not ready in hours, replace the engineer or set up your own VMs.

- Physical machines on LAN

  You may use the physical machines directly as the agent machines. This may sound like old school (no dynamic scaling or fancy technologies), but it works well for some of my clients.

Once the machine is set up, install all the necessary software to get the test scripts and run them from the command line.

- Git

---

[1]https://developer.microsoft.com/en-us/microsoft-edge/tools/vms/

- Chrome (or other browsers if necessary)

- ChromeDriver

- Test execution language runtime, e.g. Ruby

- Test libraries, e.g. Selenium-WebDriver, RSpec

  For example, if your tests are in Selenium WebDriver + RSpec, the following gems must be installed

  ```
  gem install rspec selenium-webdriver activesupport rspec_junit_formatter
  ```

  plus other support gems used in test scripts, such as `faker` and `spreadsheet`.

Decide the number of agents

I recommend starting with small and grow gradually. 3-agents is a good starting point.

Set up one build agent first. Make sure it can work with the BuildWise server to run a build. A big benefit of using VMs is easy to create clones. Once you are happy with the first agent, clone to create others. Only the config files need to be updated for different agents under the config folder (`C:/agileway/.buildwise` or `~/.buildwise`):

- `agent-config.xml`

  Most of the config items (in the configuration file) are the same across all agents.

- `agent-license.xml` (optional)

  the agent license. BuildWise agent may run in free mode for up to 45 minutes per launch.

Install BuildWise Agent

BuildWise Agents are available on Windows, macOS and Linux. Installation of BuildWise Agent is quick and straightforward:

- Windows: Run the installer and accept all default options.

- macOS: Open DMG file and drag '**BuildWise Agent**' to '**Applications**' folder.

- Linux: Run `install.sh` after unzipping the package.

As BuildWise Server is 100% open-sourced (in Ruby), software companies can develop their own agents that can work with BuildWise server.

Configure - General Settings

General   Pre-Execution   Environment Variables   Check Path

General

BuildWise Server URL   http://buildwiser.server   Visit in browser

Agent Name   Win10-Agent-04   ☑ Start Agent on Launch

Idle check interval   12 ⬍   seconds to check the BuildWise server for new builds.

Build check interval   3 ⬍   seconds to request for a new test during a build.

Target browser ⦿ Chrome   ○ Firefox   ○ IE   ○ Edge   Headless? ☐

Test results folder   C:\agileway\.buildwise\agent-test-results   Archive? ☑

Execution Path

C:\Ruby26-x64\bin;C:\Program Files\nodejs;C:\agileway\Python374\Scripts;C:\agileway\Python374;C:
\Windows\system32;C:\Windows;C:\Windows\System32\Wbem;C:\Windows
\System32\WindowsPowerShell\v1.0\;C:\Program Files\Git\cmd;C:\Program Files\Git\usr\bin;c:\apps\bin;C:
\Users\CIO\AppData\Roaming\npm

BuildWise Agent will invoke commands in the above PATH to run tests.   Check

---

- BuildWise Server URL

  The URL of the buildwise server, e.g. `http://buildwise.server`. Click the '**Visit in browser**' link to verify the connection.

- Agent Name

  The unique agent name, which is required in the server for test allocations.

- Poll intervals

  Build agents poll the CT server for a new build and the next to-be-run test script.

- Preferred browser for running tests in

  BuildWise Agent will pass an environment variable BROWSER to test execution. It is up to the test scripts to take the advantage of that.

- Test results

The directory where BuildWise agents save test results (and screenshots in case of failures) to. Tick the 'Archive test results' checkbox to retain the history of test results (in timestamped directory name) for inspection and debugging purposes.

- Execution Path

The PATH that the Agent will use to execute test scripts. BuildWise Agent provides a utility (clicking 'Check' link) to verify the software, such as Ruby and ChromeDriver (and their versions), on the agent machine.

Configure - Application

To make an agent run the tests for one build project, we need to make sure that the following two settings are in place:

- The test scripts were checked out (from Git) on the Build agent machine

This only needs to be done once. The directory must match the one set in BuildWise Project settings.

In the above example, for application **WhenWise**, its working directory on the agents can be `C:/work/whenwise` (Windows) or `/Users/zhimin/work/projects/whenwise` (macOS).

The parent repository of the checked-out project source on BuildWise Server must be the same as the one on build agents.

- Environment variables such as test server URL, ..., etc

Special environment variables are set in Agents to pass to test execution. For example, `BASE_URL` to set target server URL, so that Agent 1 $\rightarrow$ Server 1, Agent 2 $\rightarrow$ Server 2, ..., to achieve parallelism. If you can set multiple agents with the same URL, this will serve as a form of load testing as well. But the test scripts need to handle the side effects (test execution needs to be independent).

Below is an example of using `BASE_URL` in Ruby scripts.

```
def site_url(default = $BASE_URL)
   ENV['BASE_URL'] || default
end

#...
driver.get(site_url)
```

Please note that the environment variable has to be associated with an application name, so that the Agent can support multiple projects. Here is a sample configuration.

General	Pre-Execution	Environment Variables	Check Path

Defined Environment Variables

The environment variables to be passed to test execution.

TEMP	C:\TEMP		*The user-writable temporary folder used by WebDriver*

Application	Variable Name	Value
WhenWise	BASE_URL	https://ci4-whenwise.agileway.net
SupportWise	BASE_URL	https://ci4-supportwise.agileway.net
SiteWise	BASE_URL	https://ci4-sitewise.agileway.net
ClinicWise	BASE_URL	https://ci4-clinicwise.agileway.net
AgileTravel	BASE_URL	https://travel.agileway.net
TestWise	BASE	C:\agileway\TestWise6
AgileTravel-Load	BASE_URL	https://travel.agileway.net

Verify software on an Agent machine

To verify the software (and their versions) installed on the agent machine, click the **Detect** button under **Settings → Check Path**.

Verify Test Execution in an Agent

The ultimate way to verify the agent configuration is to run an actual test script, which can be triggered under the **Test Output** tab.

Configure - Pre Execution (optional)

Due to the nature of the UI test automation, unexpected situations happen (such as a browser hangs), and this may affect the next build. BuildWise Agent can be configured to run a set of pre-test-execution commands to get the machine in a ready state.

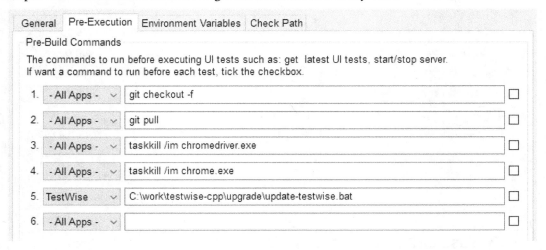

12.2 Prerequisite for Test Scripts

A set of test scripts run well on a single machine, but may not be reliable on multiple machines concurrently. The execution of the functional tests in a parallel mode must satisfy the following two requirements:

1. No execution dependencies among tests.

   Fixed execution ordering might be feasible in sequential mode, though it is still a bad practice. In a parallel mode, the execution order cannot be guaranteed. Therefore, execution dependencies are prohibited.

2. During the execution of one test script, its result must not be affected by the execution of another test at the same time.

   A better way to explain this is to show an example of two tests not meeting the requirement. Here we have two test cases:

- Test #1: User can change the Admin's password.
- Test #2: Admin user can add a new user.

Inside Test #1, there are reverse steps to set the old password back. When Test #1 and #2 are executed on a single machine, both tests will pass reliably.

However, when these two tests are running on two separate build agents (against the same test server) at the same time, Test #2 may fail. Why? If the execution of Test #2 tries to log in as Admin immediately after the password being changed by the execution of Test #1. Test #2 would fail due to "unable to login as 'admin'".

12.3 Multi-Agents against the Single Server

Many "DevOps architects" like to show off "automation on setting up server instances", such as building up a new Docker container, installing software packages and tearing down when outside office hours. With cloud scripts, it seems that setting up a server instance is easy, at least from the demo. However, in reality, many software projects I visited only had one test server instance (*dev and staging instances are not counted, as they are for different purposes*) for functional testing, and it was used for both manual testing and automated test execution.

Unless your company has a very mature deployment process, the reality is that you are only able to run automated tests against one server instance (known as 'Test server'), like below.

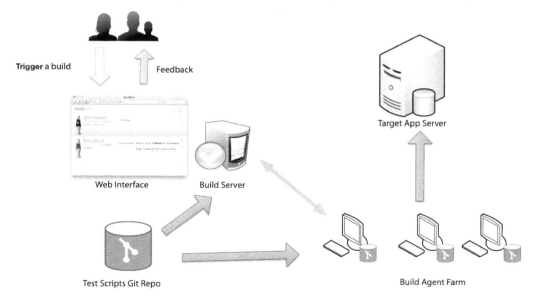

Unable to reset the database

With multiple build agents running different test scripts against the same application server, test executions #1 on one agent must not jeopardize the test executions on another. In particular, database-reset utility (*quickly reset the application data to a known state*) cannot be used in the multi-agents-one-server setup.

12.4 Multi-Agents against the Multi-Servers

To achieve the maximum CT efficiency, multi-agents-multi-servers setup shall be used. That is:

- The same software build is deployed to multiple server instances

  Automated deployment scripts must be used to ensure the exact release build is deployed on multiple servers. Because we run CT frequently, the deployment process needs to be quick.

- The build agent only executes test scripts against its assigned server instance

  e.g. Agent 1 ⇒ ci1-whenwise.agileway.net, Agent 2 ⇒ ci1-whenwise.agileway.net. This is defined at the `agent-config.xml`.

It works as below:

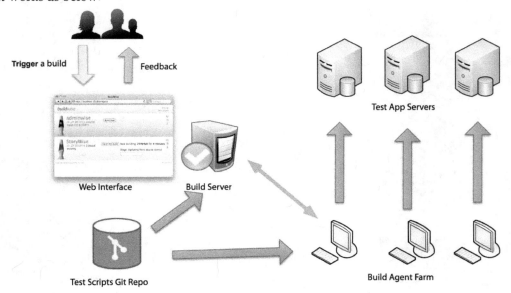

The rewards for more server instances:

- Test executions on one agent will not affect test executions on other agents
  Database-reset utility may be used.

- Scalable
  Under multi-agents-one-server setup, when the number of agents is big, the load on the single server instance will cause performance degradation. The performance degradation will affect the functional test executions, such as test failures due to timeouts for AJAX operations. In other words, there is a limit on the agent count for multi-agents-one-server setup, but not with the multi-agents-multi-servers.

For the software projects that are serious about CT (or Agile/DevOps), I would recommend this setup.

Server warm-up scripts

There shall be a process to warm up all the application servers after a new deployment. This also needs to be done in a script.

12.5 Set up a parallel build project

We need a separate build project for a parallel build on the BuildWise server. You may create one from scratch or clone from an existing one, which is easier.

Edit project: AgileTravel Sequential Build RSpec (agiletravel-quick-build-rspec)

Click the "**Duplicate**" button on an existing sequential build project, which shares the same parent Git repository.

Duplicate project: AgileTravel Sequential Build RSpec

Quickly clone an existing build project, you may customize the setting later.

New Project Name:	AgileTravel Parallel Build RSpec
New Project Identifier:	agiletravel-parallel-build-rspec
Test Execution Mode:	○ **Sequential** ◉ **Parallel**
App name	AgileTravel
Work directory on Agents:	/Users/zhimin/work/projects/agiletravel-ui-tests;C:/work/agiletravel-ui-tests
UI Test Task:	-f selenium-webdriver-rspec/Rakefile ci:ui_tests:full
Branch:	default to master

[Clone] [Cancel]

- Test Execution Mode
  Set to "**Parallel**".

- App name
  This identifies the application (defined in BuildWise agents) to test. This is mandatory.

- Work directory on Agents
  The checked-out working directories (from the same parent repository) on the agents.
  You can specify a set of paths for different OS platforms, separated by `;`.

- UI Test Task
  The Rake task name will be different from the one for the sequential build. The default
  `ci:ui_tests:full`, included in sample Rakefile, shall be good for most projects. As
  always, you have the freedom to customize.

12.6 Monitor the build progress

After a parallel build is started (*the same way as triggering a sequential build*), you will be
redirected to the build page where you will see the following:

1. A list of test script files

AGENT	TEST FILE (0 test cases)	TIME (S)	RESULT
	03_passenger_spec.rb 📄		73
	04_payment_spec.rb 📄		17
	01_login_spec.rb 📄		4
	02_flight_spec.rb 📄		1

2. Build agents start to 'pick up' a test script (to run)

AGENT	TEST FILE (0 test cases)	TIME (S)	RESULT
Win10-Agent-04	03_passenger_spec.rb 📄		73
Mac-Agent-00	04_payment_spec.rb 📄		17
	01 login spec.rb 📄		4

3. Test results are sent back from the agents

Win10-Agent-04	03_passenger_spec.rb 📄		Rerun	73
Mac-Agent-00	04_payment_spec.rb 📄 💬 Output	11.6		17
	- Payment [5] Book flight with payment	5.9	OK	

4. A test is being auto-retried on another agent

The test 03_passenger failed on the agent 'Win10-Agent-04' first, then was retried on another agent, 'Mac-Agent-00', in this case.

Mac-Agent-00 (Win10-Agent-04)	03_passenger_spec.rb 📄 💬	23.7		73
	- Passenger [4] Can enter passenger details (using page objects)	5.0	Failure	📷

5. A completed parallel build

12.7 Assess the benefits of parallelism

Some astute readers might find that there were no real benefits (actually it was slightly slower with the parallel build) in the above example. The reason was that there was overhead with parallel execution, such as test allocations and waiting intervals on the agents. In the above same build, when executing a regression suite of 6 simple selenium tests with 2 agents, the overhead outweighs the benefits.

Now let me show you a real parallel build report to explain the two main benefits of parallelism in CT:

- **Time-saving**

  For the above build, 4.5 hours of execution time is reduced to 51 minutes, a save of **80%** time with 6 agents.

- **Reliability**

  More importantly, the auto-retry feature (I will cover this in the next chapter) of BuildWise will make CT builds much more reliable. For this build, 9 out of 444 tests failed on one agent, but then passed on another agent. Those 9 failures were false-alarms, i.e.the failures are not real functional issues but unreliable execution ones such as not waiting long enough for an AJAX operation to complete (which are very common in a dynamic web app)

	Duration: **51 minutes**	Time saved by parallel: **80.6%**	False alarms: 9

ted: **2020-09-08 10:21**

False alarms

Test file	Failed on	Passed on
business_promotion_voucher_spec.rb	Linux-Agent-06	Win10-Agent-04
business_type_calendar_spec.rb	Win10-Agent-04	Win10-Agent-01

If you have worked on CT, you will know this is a big benefit.

12.8 Common Issues

1. ChromeDriver is not installed or not in the PATH

   No Chrome browser starts up, all tests failed after around 20 seconds.

   Test Output: (*click "Failure" to view*)

   ```
   Selenium::WebDriver::Error::WebDriverError:
   unable to connect to chromedriver 127.0.0.1:9515
   ```

   Fix: Verify the `chromedriver` in BuildWise Agent's **Settings**.

   A special note for rbenv users. Installing/Updating some libraries might create `/Users/YOU/.rbenv/shims/chromedriver`, which might be invalid and precede the working one. The workaround is to simply delete `/Users/YOU/.rbenv/shims/chromedriver` or make it a symbolic link to the correct one such as `/usr/local/bin/chromedriver`.

2. The 'Work directory on Agents' specified in the project settings does not match the one on the agents

   All test script files listed on BuildWise server's build page, but no single test picked up by the agents.

   Check the log (under **Log** tab) on the BuildWise Agent. Below is an example of a typo in the path.

```
[ WARN] AgileTravel's checked out directory: /Users/me/work/projects/
        Zagiletravel-ui-tests;C:/work/agiletravel-ui-tests
        not exists on the agent machine
```

Fix: Update the correct path in the project setting.

3. The App name set in the project settings is not supported by the agents.

   All test script files listed on BuildWise server's build page, but no single test picked up by the agents.

   Check the `log/buildwise_agent.log`, it might contain:

```
[Warning] The agent does not support App: AgileTravel-New, ignore!
```

   Fix: Update the correct path in the project setting.

4. Test execution failed, due to missing dependent key libraries

   The agent is running a test (shown on BuildWise server), but it seemed stuck.

   Check the log (under **Log** tab) on the BuildWise Agent.

```
[ INFO] Execute test: 03_passenger_spec.rb
[ WARN] Test result xml file /Users/me/.buildwise/agent-test-results/SPEC.result.xml
        not found
```

   Verify: (under 'Test Ouptut' tab)

```
Gem::MissingSpecError:
  Could not find 'rspec_junit_formatter' (>= 0) among 572 total gem(s)
{format: text}
```

   Fix: Install the missing library.

13. Parallel Test Execution Best Practices

Parallel testing in CT does not simply mean throwing in more build machines, far from that. With more build machines involved, the complexity of CT grows significantly. In this chapter, I will share some of the best practices that I have learned in parallel test execution in CT. These practices are generally applicable to other CT servers. I will use BuildWise as an example here, so that you can follow the instructions and put them into practice (at home or work).

13.1 Optimal agent count

Some architects and managers got excited at seeing parallel execution of automated UI tests (in BuildWise) for the first time. They said: "*That's great! We will set up hundreds of agents, it shall not be hard with AWS ...*". It is wrong. The testing infrastructure shall be based on realistic needs, not a sound-good plan. More build machines means more cost. I will cover more in the next chapter, "Parallel testing lab".

The optimal agent count is set by your desired build time. For example, suppose the average execution time of your regression test suite is 1.5 hours, and you would like "10-minute build" *(an Extreme Programming practice)*. In that case, ten build machines are enough: `1.5 * 60 / 10` plus overhead (of parallel execution).

For most software projects, 10 build machines shall be enough, considering the following factors:

- The size of the regression test suite

  If you only have 40 selenium tests and the test automation engineers struggled with test maintenance, there is no point in building a 50-agent parallel testing lab. Seeking help from a qualified test automation coach first in this case.

- Infrastructure Cost

  This includes hardware purchases or hosting fees and software licences.

- Load on the server

  Is your app server capable of handling the load generated from parallel test executions? In a few projects I have consulted, with a complex deployment process (commonly using a number of Docker containers), the mini 3-agent parallel testing lab on my laptop sometimes brought the server to its knees.

- Infrastructure maintenance efforts

  If you go for multi-agent-multi-server topology, adding one extra agent means a new server environment!

Like many decisions on test automation and CT, if you don't spend too much time on making big plans, you will find that the correct approach is right there, intuitive, affordable and flexible to grow. For the number of build agents, just start with small: 3-agent is a good starting point. Once the execution time exceeds your ideal build time with a growing number of tests, add more agents. By then, the experiences you have gained would help you make better adjustments if needed, rather than spending hours and hours on meetings.

13.2 Intelligent test execution ordering

Intelligent test execution ordering is a CT technique that dynamically re-arranges the test execution order based on the past execution results of individual test scripts, in hope of running recently failed tests first. While this does not reduce the overall execution time, it will reduce the team's "waiting time" for "interested" test executions.

Intelligent test execution ordering is also a best practice for sequential builds which I covered in Chapter 11. In the parallel testing mode, intelligent test execution ordering is more flexible.

1. Intelligent test execution ordering is enabled by default

   In the parallel testing mode, the execution order means the order a CT server assigns to participated build agents (on a first-come-first-serve basis). There is no point to expect certain test execution sequences, as the execution order (among all the agents) cannot be guaranteed (and every test script must be independent).

   ◆ UI Test Results (0 tests)

AGENT	TEST FILE (0 test cases)	TIME (S)	RESULT
Win10-Agent-04	invoicing_payment_remove_payment_item_spec.rb 📄	49	
Win10-Agent-05	invoicing_payment_apply_uninvoiced_payment_item_spec.rb 📄	48	
Linux-Agent-06	holiday_branch_spec.rb 📄	42	

2. Manual override test priority

   You can set the priority of a test script at any time during a CT build. In BuildWise, you may click the test priority number next to a test script to update its priority for the current build.

13.3 Auto retry failed tests once more

Back in 2006, after the automated test suite (in Watir) grew to a certain size (I don't remember the test count, but about 30-min execution time), we found ourselves spending more and more time dealing with the false alarms (test failures not caused by a functional defect). I couldn't find any solutions, so I came up with 'Auto-Retry' approach and implemented it as a plugin to the CI Server (CruiseControl). It worked very well. In my opinion, it is a must-have feature for CT.

As we know, automated UI tests are far more brittle than unit tests, for the reasons below:

- dynamic operation (AJAX or JS)

- a dependent service is down or suddenly being slow

- the server is under load.

- hardware or network issues

The above may happen at any time. The most common false alarm is "the test script didn't wait long enough for an AJAX operation to complete". As we all know, one failed test means the whole CT build failed. No matter how much more time/effort we spent on stabilising test scripts, it is still an impossible mission to prevent a single false alarm for a large test suite (like WhenWise regression test suite, 25002 test steps in 482 selenium tests).

In my opinion, there is only one practical solution: Auto-retry. In a parallel build, the CT server automatically assigns a failed test to another build agent to run, to give it one more chance. It works as below:

1. Test #87 failed on Agent 1, the result was sent to the CT server

2. CT server put Test #87 into 'waiting to be run' queue, waiting for the next available agent

3. Agent 3 picked up Test #87 and ran it.

   - failed again
     CT server 'thinks' the test failed.

   - pass.
     CT server 'thinks' the test passed, and the previous failure was a 'false alarm'.

I don't recommend Auto-Retry for the sequential build, as it wouldn't help to detect issues with hardware, network, software (e.g. browser version) and test scripts (failed to update). After all, when the regression test suite reaches a certain size, they have to be run in parallel anyway.

Don't add auto-retry in your test scripts

I noticed 'auto-retry' feature has recently been added to some 'new test frameworks', such as Jest and Cypress. Here is an example.

```
jest.retryTimes(3) //set maximum retries number

describe('Test', () => {
    test('Test_Test', async () => {
        //test code
        ...
    })
})
```

It is wrong! An 'Auto-Retry' shall be applied by the Continuous Testing Server, not fiddling with test scripts. An immediate auto-retry on a failed step won't be of much help (only a little), simply pushing its luck. As a matter of fact, it will add more complexity to the test scripts, and may lead to bad practices such as "too many retries", which will slow down the test execution. For example, a lazy engineer might just blindly increase retry times to hope for stable test executions.

13.4 Manually rerun a failed test

While Auto-Retry is very useful, sometimes it might not be enough, especially with a large regression suite. For example, a test script failed due to a connection timed out error (`Net::ReadTimeout with #<TCPSocket:(closed)>` for RSpec tests) when the server was under the load, and the subsequent retry on another agent could fail too. When the server is back to a healthy state, you may trigger a manual rerun of this test (like below), which would be put back into 'the waiting to be run' queue.

Linux-Agent-06 (*Win10-Agent-05*)	invoicing_payment_apply_uninvoiced_payment_item_spec.rb	31.5	Rerun	48
	- Invoicing - Payment - Apply invoiced payment item Apply previous payment item back to the same invoice	10.9	Failure	
	- Invoicing - Payment - Apply invoiced payment item Apply previous payment item back to another invoice	8.1	Failure	

With a large regression test suite (e.g. over 500 Selenium tests), manual runs are required for most CT builds.

13.5 Cross-Platform Testing

We may use multiple build agents on different platforms (Windows, macOS and Linux) to participate in one CT build in BuildWise. The setup of cross-platform testing (testing one app on multiple platforms) is simple in BuildWise: specify the paths of the checked-out work directory on the agent machines.

App name *	AgileTravel
Work directory on Agents *	/Users/zhimin/work/projects/agiletravel-ui-tests; C:/work/agiletravel-ui-tests; /home/zhimin/work/agiletravel-ui-tests

In the above, three work paths are:

- (macOS): `/Users/zhimin/work/projects/agiletravel-ui-tests`

- (Windows): `C:/work/agiletravel-ui-tests`

- (Linux): `/home/zhimin/work/agiletravel-ui-tests`

13.6 Headless or not?

A headless browser is a web browser without a graphical user interface. The supposed benefits of headless browser testing are

- **Faster**

  Based on my benchmark test (2017), ChromeDriver runs ∼20% faster with a small set of selenium tests in headless mode.

- **Less distraction**

  Test execution is in a 'stealth' mode.

Chrome (since v59) makes real headless testing possible. However, please be aware that there may be limitations with headless mode, for instance, chromedriver's early versions did not work with browser-window sizing-related tests.

I prefer executing tests in a visible browser window, as viewing test executions can help me to improve test scripts. For example, an error stack trace is shown in the browser but not checked in the test script. In terms of performance, running tests in multiple build agents concurrently offers much better performance gains, plus execution reliability.

Fake Headless testing with PhantomJS between 2011-2017

Prior to the introduction of headless mode in Chrome (v59), PhantomJS was the hyped headless implementation. I tried and was not impressed, as I wrote down in my 'Selenium WebDriver Recipes in Ruby' book (2014): "*I am not a big fan of headless testing with browser simulation*". I have never seen one successful implementation of headless testing using PhantomJS, but it seemed that most test architects and tech leads talked about it frequently. Three years later (2017), the maintainer of PhantomJS deprecated it. He posted this[*]: "*I think people will switch to it, eventually. Chrome is faster and more stable than PhantomJS. And it doesn't eat memory like crazy.*" In other words, all those claimed headless web test automation turned out to be all fake, as the execution is not even stable, according to the PhantomJS developers.

I respect the programmers behind PhantomJS. Unfortunately, PhantomJS has been misused by some tech leads to fake their knowledge in test automation.

ᵃhttps://groups.google.com/forum/m/#!topic/phantomjs/9aI5d-LDuNE

13.7 Distribution rules

Ideally, each test script in a regression test suite is completely independent and runs the same on every build agent. While these may be achieved at a cost, some compromises may be made by applying some rules to how the test scripts assigned to the build agents.

- A certain tests might be only performed on a specific agent

  For example, only one build agent machine has licensed software that can verify PDF documents. Therefore, all PDF-checking tests shall be run on that agent machine.

- A set of test scripts must be executed on the same agent

  If two tests cannot be run at the same time (may cause conflicts) on different build agents, one workaround is to add a rule to make them run on the same agent.

The distribution rules can be set for a BuildWise project.

Distribution rules	Test Files	Rule	Agents	Active?	
+ Add rule	["access_check_spec.rb","access_check_staff_spec.rb"]	only_on_agents	["Linux-Agent-02"]	☑	🗑
	["biz_change_start_minutes_spec.rb","biz_client_spec.rb"]	on_same_agent		☑	🗑

13.8 Delay completion

With a large End-2-End test suite, getting all tests pass (green build) is not a trivial effort. A green build means each of every test step passed. If the last test failed, before its second chance (i.e. Auto-Retry), the while build failed. If it was a false alarm, CT engineers could get quite frustrated.

This issue started bothering me back in 2007. I came up with a solution, inspired by the lifts I saw in Taiwan. I found there was a 'Hold Open' button in many lifts there. If this button was pressed, the lift doors kept open. I implemented this idea in BuildWise so that CT engineers may delay the completion of a build.

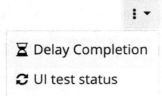

So that they can let Auto-Retry complete and apply 'Manual Rerun' if necessary.

When it is ready, click the 'Continue' button in the top banner to resume.

14. Parallel Testing Lab

A CT lab (also known as build farm or grid) consists of one CT server and a set of build agents to execute automated functional tests. Compared to other testing infrastructure setups such as manual testing lab, load testing lab and CI setup for executing automated unit tests, the requirement for a CT lab is much higher:

- High reliability

  As required for functional testing. Automated GUI tests are known for being brittle.

- Long execution time

  Functional test execution, in terms of execution time, is 100x or 1000x of unit test execution.

- Large scale

  To keep short build time with a growing functional test suite, a significant investment in the infrastructure is required.

- High importance

  The whole team, often the executives as well, are interested in the results of a CT build (run in a CT lab), as it decides whether a software build fits for a production release.

Google's Test Lab

Partick Copeland, Google's Senior Engineering Director, talked about Google's CI and test lab in one interview (Testing the limits[a]) in 2010:

- 5000 CPU cores

- over 100M executed test suites (*I think most of them are unit tests*)

- annual growth rate of 75%

- average build and test cycle take just 4 minutes

In this chapter, I will share my experiences in setting up parallel testing labs for executing a large number of automated functional tests.

14.1 Hosting option: Cloud-based or On-premises?

A CT lab can be set up either on cloud-based infrastructure (e.g. AWS) or on-premises. Many people would assume that "Cloud" will be a natural selection, as it sounds 'cool'. However, for most companies, it is often not the best option. There are many benefits to go for setting up an on-premise CT lab:

- Behind the firewall, no VPN/tunnels are required

- Low latency

  Quick feedback is important in CT, any saving on speed is welcome.

- Lower cost (most likely)

  The hosting fee for an individual cloud instance is not high, but when all are added-together with a large number of machines (which can well be the case for a CT lab), the monthly AWS bill can be quite alarming.

- Faster test execution

  You can customize the best VM settings that will work best for test execution.

- Security

  All data resides in the company network. For security-sensitive organisations, the cloud-based setup might not be feasible anyway.

- Flexible

  You are in control.

- Avoid complications

  Some network engineers, usually incompetent ones, went too far with IAAS, resulting in unreliable infrastructure.

- Avoid political impacts

  There are a lot of hypes and emerging new technologies on IAAS. I have seen cases of switching AWS to Azure, Docker to Kubernetes in some companies, not much for technical reasons, more about a change of senior management. Remember, the actual requirement for the agent machines for a CT lab is very basic: make it like an end-user's machine.

- Avoid planning big

  Excessive plannings in most software activities are often unnecessary (*the spirit of Agile*). Besides wasting the time, a side-effect is that it prevents people from doing real stuff. At large organisations, I often heard "*'Test Automation' is a sensitive term*". Why? There was a big picture painted by the CIO, but it failed embarrassingly.

  A useful parallel testing lab can be set up on the first day, without dependencies and at virtually no cost. The team can grow as needed. If the direction is set for cloud-based by the management, this option won't exist.

For a large organisation whose infrastructure is already on the cloud, with a team of really competent cloud engineers, a good cloud-based parallel testing lab can be achieved as well.

14.2 Cost

Frankly, money can be a deciding factor for a parallel testing lab. Most executives do not mind throwing millions of dollars for a proof of concept (POC) to try test automation or CT. However, they are not keen on paying for a parallel testing lab, for the reasons below:

- On-going effort

  CT Lab is not a once-off project. There will be a dedicated and on-going budget for a parallel testing lab.

- Avoid embarrassments

  Failing POC is not a problem at all. However, it would be hard for a CIO to acknowledge that a parallel testing lab is no longer needed as the test automation has failed.

- Lack of confidence in technical capability

- Fear of change

  If it does work, can the teams cope with the feedback (detected defects)?

Putting the office politics aside, the cost of :

- Hardware

  Physical or virtual machines.

- Hosting fee, if hosted externally

- OS Licenses

  For agents that run Microsoft Windows, you need to pay for the OS licenses.

- Agent licenses

- Any other software licenses required on the build agents

"Developer efficiency is the key thing that your infrastructure teams should be striving for, and this is why at Facebook, we have some of our top engineers working on developer infrastructure" - Katie Coons, the software engineer of Product Stability at Facebook, presentation "Big Code: Developer Infrastructure at Facebook's Scale[1]" at F8 conference in 2015 (*at 45:34*)

Apart from the cost of physical resources and licenses, the biggest cost is actually staffing. You need to put your best engineers to work on it, just like what Facebook did. I know some readers, such as many senior executives, find it hard to comprehend. Let me ask you this question: "For a new employee, how long did it take to get the machine set up correctly with all the access?" From my experiences at large organizations, it normally takes a few days. A build agent is just like an 'end-user'. In a CT lab, the efforts of setting up all 'test users' are nothing compared to other work CT engineers do every day, such as:

- Maintain all software

  For example, Chrome browser self-updates about every 2 months. When it happens, CT engineers need to update build machines with an updated ChromeDriver as well.

- Inspect test failures

  CT engineers cannot simply inform the developers of every test failure on a CT build, as it could be environment-related. For example, a new library was added in test scripts. In this case, CT engineers need to update all build machines. In other words, a good CT engineer is also a good test automation engineer.

---

[1] https://www.youtube.com/watch?t=1896&v=X0VH78ye4yY

14.3 Advice: starting small, grow gradually

Once you have decided on the hosting option, make it happen by starting small. I suggest 1 server + 3 agents, i.e., four VMs in total. At some companies, the process of getting VMs can take quite a while. You may set up one mini CT lab on a laptop computer (I often got it done on my first day of consulting) using VirtualBox (a free VM software from Oracle).

The fact is that real functional test automation and CT are extremely rare. The outcomes of a series of meetings by a group of managers and technical architects, from my observations, were always wrong. The reason was obvious. The concept of Agile or Test Automation or CI was not new. If these worked well, the management shall not need to meet to decide what approach to implementing them now. More meetings won't help test automation and CT.

Without strong support from a chief executive, the only practical way is to "show and tell". Do CT in your team first. Start with a small CT lab, and grow gradually. Upon seeing the real benefits of running automated UI tests daily, people may change.

14.4 My preferred setup for CT Lab

Both BuildWise server and BuildWise agents run on all major desktop platforms: Windows, macOS, and Linux. There are no server-agent pair restrictions. For web app testing, what matters to test execution the most is the browser (Chrome with chromedriver, Firefox with geckodriver, ..., etc).

Operating Systems

- BuildWise Server - macOS

  BuildWise server runs fine on Windows Server as well. However, the application server is usually better on Unix-based OS such as macOS and Linux. I prefer macOS over Linux for one reason: when executing UI test sequentially (run in the server), Chrome setup on macOS is easier.

- Build Agent - 1 macOS, 1 Windows and multiple Linux agents

  A Linux build agent VM requires less CPU/RAM resources. It is faster than Windows VM and completely free in terms of OS licenses.

On-premise build agent machines

I prefer using Mac mini computers as the build agent machines (*Facebook use Mac minis too*) for its size, quietness, build quality and performance. The new Apple Mac mini with M1 is very fast, it is on par with some Intel-based high-end desktop computers according to some reviews.

You may run Windows on Intel-based Mac mini computers, using VM software such as VMware Fusion and Parallels Desktop.

14.5 Set up BuildWise Server

In the previous chapters, I have covered the setup of a BuildWise CT server. You do the same for a CT lab.

- Run BuildWise in production mode with MySQL database backend.

- You may run BuildWise server in Linux/macOS and agents in Windows.

- A dedicated database server (MySQL) shall be used for a large CT lab.

Run BuildWise Server on HTTPS

BuildWise server is a Sinatra (a lightweight web framework in Ruby) app. Sinatra Apps can be run with Nginx or Apache2, and the easiest way is to use Phusion Passenger[2]. If an app runs in Nginx or Apache2, then a competent network administrator can configure it to fit any organisations.

Here are sample configurations for BuildWise server running in Nginx and Apache2 (SSL) with Passenger.

- **Nginx**

  Passenger configuration in *nginx.conf*:

---

[2]https://www.phusionpassenger.com/

```
http {
 passenger_max_pool_size 24;
 passenger_pool_idle_time 10;

 passenger_root /opt/.rbenv/versions/2.6.4/lib/ruby/gems/2.6.0/gems/passenger-6.0.3;
 passenger_ruby /opt/.rbenv/versions/2.6.4/bin/ruby;

 #...
 include /opt/etc/nginx/sites-enabled/*;
}
```

Virtual host for BuildWise server (listening on port 80):

```
server {
  listen        80;
  server_name   buildwise.macmini;
  root /opt/www/sinatra/buildwise/public;
  passenger_enabled on;
  passenger_min_instances 1;
  rails_env production;
}
```

- **Apache2**

  Loading Passenger module in *apache2.conf.*

  ```
  LoadModule passenger_module /.../passenger-6.0.3/buildout/apache2/mod_passenger.so
  <IfModule mod_passenger.c>
   PassengerRoot /opt/.rbenv/versions/2.6.4/lib/ruby/gems/2.6.0/gems/passenger-6.0.3
   PassengerDefaultRuby /opt/.rbenv/versions/2.6.4/bin/ruby
  </IfModule>
  ```

  Virtual host for BuildWise server (listening on port 443):

```
<VirtualHost *:443>
  ServerName buildwise.server
  DocumentRoot  /var/www/sinatra/buildwise/public
  RackEnv production

  SSLEngine On
  SSLCertificateFile    /etc/apache2/ssl/buildwise_server_.crt
  SSLCertificateKeyFile /etc/apache2/ssl/buildwise_server_.key
  SSLCertificateChainFile /etc/apache2/ssl/gd_bundle.crt

  # ...
</VirtualHost>
```

14.6 Set up Build Agents

The setup of a build agent, as I have covered in a previous chapter, is quite simple. To minimize the efforts, do spend time to get the first one done correctly, then clone it to create others.

Name machine well

Name build agent machine in a way that it is easy to identify, such as Win10-Agent-01 and Linux-Agent-02.

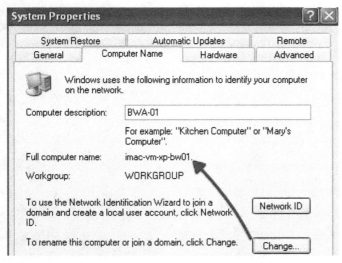

Set up Git Authentication

We want to the build agents to run latest test scripts, which means, the agent machine can update the test scripts from the parent repository, i.e. `git pull` for Git. By default, authentication is required for a Git operation. We need to set up Git authentication so that no credentials prompts for the build agents.

SSH without password for macOS/Linux

Generate a pair of RSA authentication keys in $\sim$/.ssh, if you haven't got them already.

```
~> ssh-keygen -t rsa
```

Run the command below to

```
~> cat ~/.ssh/id_rsa.pub | ssh b@B 'cat >> .ssh/authorized_keys'
```

Verify. You shall be able to log into B as b from A as a without a password:

```
~> ssh b@B
```

SSH without password on Windows

Make sure HOME environment variable is set. To verify, run

```
> echo %HOME%
```

to set

Open Git Bash.

1. Generate SSH key pairs

   ```
   > ssh-keygen -t rsa
   ```

   Follow the prompt (just press Enter key).

   Your identification has been saved in /c/Users/Administrator/.ssh/id_rsa.
   Your public key has been saved in /c/Users/Administrator/.ssh/id_rsa.pub.

2. Copy the public key to the build server machine, add to 'authorized_keys'

   Copy the .ssh/id_rsa.pub file to the target machine, e.g. macmini, the CT server machine.

   ```
   > cat build_machine_1_id_rsa.pub  >> ~/.ssh/authorized_keys
   ```

3. Try out

   ```
   > ssh macmini -l zhimin
   ```

You shall be able to log in to (with the username you will use to check out from Git repository) the CT server machine without prompting for a password.

 If the remote machine is a Mac, you must turn on "Remote Login" in Settings.

Set up a working folder on Build Agents

Select a folder (I use `C:/work`) on the build agent machine as the working folder. Clone the project (containing the test scripts) from the parent repository.

```
> cd work
> git clone zhimin@macmini:/var/repos/whenwise.git
```

Verify that you can update the scripts.

```
> cd work\whenwise
> git pull
```

14.7 Best Practices

My following recommendations are limited to my experiences with only small-to-medium (up to 25 agents) parallel testing labs.

Make your agent machine fast and reliable

When a good CT process is in place, the machines (both the server and the agents) in the test lab are probably the most hard-working ones in your company. It makes good business sense to use decent hardware for the build machines. The cost of unreliable test executions (caused by hardware failures/slowness) is high. CT engineers need to investigate every test failure, spending a bit extra on high-quality hardware is the most economical way to minimize that.

Uses logic server names defined in the hosts file

Build agents communicate with the CT server, target app server and maybe supporting services (e.g. mail server). To make the build agent configuration is more resilient to changes, it might be a good idea to add a layer of abstraction: instead of hard coding server IP address, use a logic name that defined in the hosts file, as the example below:

```
192.168.1.15 buildwise.server
192.168.1.15 mail.server
192.168.1.23 ci1-whenwise.agileway.net
192.168.1.24 ci2-whenwise.agileway.net
```

The hosts file is located under /etc/hosts on Linux and macOS;
C:\Windows\System32\drivers\etc\hosts on Windows.

Ideally make the agents the same specification

This will help to flag the performance issues. If the execution of one test script takes a noticeable longer time than the previous builds, it might be due to a recent bad check-in. By running all tests on the same hardware specification, it will be easier to make a call on that.

Site License for Dynamic Scaling

If you have a good Cloud engineer, implementing a parallel testing lab with dynamic scaling is possible. This sounds cool. However, it may not be easy, because every agent configuration, including all the software licenses on the machine, cannot be tied to a named machine.

BuildWise agent offers a site license that will use the machine IP address as the agent name, so that you may spin up a large number of licensed build agents as needed.

Prefer Linux/Mac over Windows

On VMs with similar resources, test executions on Linux are faster than Windows (*around 20%, based on the results of my test lab*) . Test executions on macOS are quite fast too. Because I ran BuildWise agents on macOS natively, I don't have a meaningful comparison against two other platforms.

Another advantage with Linux is that the OS is free, with no license fees. You may add more build agents by simply cloning the build agent VM images, without worrying about licensing.

Be aware of limitations

There are thousands of build machines in Facebook and Google test labs. Don't be that ambitious, especially for those CIOs who want to appear cool in public talks. My advice is to **grow as needed**. After the test lab reaches a certain size, a reduction of 10% execution time might cost 100% more in terms of resources and efforts.

If you are using BuildWise, the solution is limited to AgileWay CT Grading 4 (see Chapter 6). That is about a suite of 1000 end-to-end UI tests. More tests means more agents are required, therefore, the communication to the server might be a bottleneck. Frankly, I have never run more than 25 BuildWise agents. If you plan a large testing lab, I recommend this great Facebook presentation on CI[3], the engineer mentioned "Distributed Queueing" to solve the growing issue. It made sense to me, but I have no ideas on how to implement it yet.

Time-box the set up in days, not months

Quite often, the set-up of a test tab in a large organisation involves many meetings and approvals. In a recent project, the so-called 'long-term strategy' has changed 3 times within 2 months: self-host VM -> AWS -> Azure. However, that did not affect my team. We have been running BuildWise with 3 VirtualBox VMs since day 1. The tech lead and manager were in and out of different meetings, occasionally with some news. Upon leaving the project, I still haven't got access to one VM on an agreed 'long-term strategy'.

14.8 Wrap up

Setting up a large parallel testing lab to be used by all the software projects in the company, like Facebook and Google, is a good idea, as it maximizes the use of resources. However, don't underestimate the political challenges without strong support from the top executives. I would recommend projects setting up one just for its own use first. The team has the freedom to choose the best technology stack that is suitable. As you have seen, it is easy to start with a mini testing lab (1 server + 3 agents) with a very low investment in both cost and efforts. And it can usually be done within hours. Grow it as needed. While quick feedback is essential in CT, the quality of the feedback is more important. False alarms will destroy the developers' confidence in CT. Without trust, there will be no CT. Hence, no DevOps or Agile.

---

[3]https://www.youtube.com/watch?t=1896&v=X0VH78ye4yY

15. Why do most projects fail in CT?

Test Automation and Continuous Testing are not borderline impossible, but simply very easy to get wrong! - Zhimin Zhan

A successful CT process requires high quality of each of its components:

- Test Automation
- Infrastructure
- Continuous Execution

In other words, if any one of the three components is unsatisfactory, the CT process fails. Besides the above technical aspects, there are also human factors.

15.1 Failure Factors - test automation

A fact: few software engineers (in Test) received proper education or training in test automation, which is unfortunate. Considering this: commonly, 30-40% members of a software team are testers, in addition to full-time testers, programmers and business analysts spend a lot of time performing functional testing as well. However, to my knowledge, there are no Functional Testing courses taught at universities. Not surprisingly, many wrong decisions on test automation are made due to a lack of knowledge.

Wrong choice of automation framework

This is the most frustrating area in my over 14 years of consulting in test automation. Managers or architects often make wrong decisions, while a correct approach ticks all the boxes. I quoted Microsoft's recommendation earlier. If one of the largest software companies in the world states "*Our (test automation) software was not good and will abolish it, we recommend X*". And X is free and a standard, it should be no brainer, right? However, the reality is far from common sense.

Here are two forms of how Software projects chose a wrong automation framework:

- **Tool-based**, commonly with record-n-playback

  Record-n-playback tools have been long existed in software testing, with bad reputations. At every software testing conference I attended, the general response to those record/playback tools is 'NO'. However, new record/playback test automation framework/tools come and go in a slightly different form, such as RFT, QTP/UFT, Ranorex, Sahi, TestComplete and Cypress. To me, the recording-based approach is fundamentally wrong, because the most effort of test automation is in test maintenance, and recorded test scripts are hard to maintain.

  > *Record/Playback scripts are notoriously costly from a maintenance perspective.* -
  > 'Agile Testing' book on page 315

  To my knowledge, every project using one of those record-n-playback tools failed test automation badly.

- **'self-created framework'** on top of Selenium WebDriver

  Have you seen "building test automation frameworks from scratch" on Job Ads for Test Automation Engineer? I saw a lot in Australia. There are many "Automation Framework design" tutorials on YouTube. The fact is that the engineers (such as Simon Stewart, the creator of Selenium WebDriver) who can create a high-quality automation framework from scratch are extremely rare. These engineers are most likely unavailable on the job market.

  I have consulted in a few projects with the so-called 'own test automation framework'. To give you a feel for how bad things could be? Two projects had to create a separate defect tracking for their own test automation framework! Those 'frameworks' added a badly-implemented layer of abstraction on top of the Selenium WebDriver, and the unnecessary abstraction layers were based on the misunderstandings of test automation, which were often inspired by some record-n-playback tools.

  Not surprisingly, test automation with 'own-framework' failed, not only at the technical aspect but also with subtle human factors. The embarrassment will prevent the management (who made the wrong call) from adopting the correct test automation framework: raw Selenium WebDriver.

In my opinion, raw Selenium WebDriver is the easiest-to-learn automation framework, because its syntax follows an intuitive pattern: **Locate a control then Drive it**. For example:

```
driver.find_element(:link_text, "Login").click
driver.find_element(:id, "username").send_keys("agileway")
driver.find_element(:name,"password").clear
driver.find_element(:xpath,"//input[@value='Sign In']").click
puts driver.find_element(:tag, "body").text
```

The equivalent of the above in Java:

```
driver.findElement(By.linkText("Login")).click();
driver.findElement(By.id("username")).send_keys("agileway");
driver.findElement(By.name("password")).clear();
driver.findElement(By.xpath("//input[@value='Sign In']")).click();
System.out.println(driver.findElement(By.tagName("body")).getText());
```

Selenium WebDriver is the easist-to-learn automation framework

I have conducted many in-house Selenium WebDriver training sessions, nearly everyone (most are manual testers) was able to use Selenium WebDriver for work the next day. Here I will emphasize, we use raw Selenium WebDriver in RSpec. I know this might contradict some readers' perceptions. In fact, during my one-day training (some call it workshop, as attendants do hands-on testing), I spent half the time on maintainable test design. There is really not much on Selenium WebDriver syntax (as you have seen in the above sample scripts), because it is so simple and logical. During my training, every attendant will develop 6 test cases from scratch, and then refactor them into page objects.

If there is a secret in my training, it is the combination of using TestWise IDE and carefully selected examples. TestWise IDE keeps the attendants focused on writing test scripts (*raw Selenium*), they learn quickly from immediate feedback. Quick satisfaction brings enjoyment, which further increases learning efficiency. I have seen one Selenium tutoring video on YouTube, the instructor spent about a half-hour on installing Java, selenium libraries and how to use Eclipse, which many manual testers will feel overwhelmed.

Why do many companies use 'selenium webdriver is hard to learn' as the excuse for choosing a bad (and expensive) test automation framework/tool?

- Architects have little knowledge and no hands-on experience in test automation
  Let's face it, Software Engineers in Test were not treated seriously in most software companies (the exceptions are in the world's leading IT firms). Often, when a new test automation attempt is initiated, the people who are making technical decisions often are technical architects and principal software engineers, not test engineers.

- Unable to blame if choosing a free and open-source framework

  Many software engineers never saw one successful implementation of UI test automation. Failure is the word they associate with automated functional testing. If one technical architect was put in a position to choose a test automation solution, he tends to vote for a "safe" (for him, no the company) one. *"If I chose an IBM testing tool when it fails, it is IBM's fault. If I chose Selenium WebDriver, when it fails, people will question my ability"*.

- Favour the 'hyped' technologies

  When one person has no ideas, he tends to follow what seems to be 'cool stuff', such as BDD, Cloud-based, Cross-browser testing, Headless mode, ..., etc.

- Resume-driving testing

  Some engineers, with very limited knowledge in test automation, think they can build a 'new framework' that offers better efficiency. They want "designed a new test automation framework" in their resumes.

- Favour solutions with 'comfortable technologies'

  For example, A technical architect often only programmed in one compiled language such as Java and C#, he probably would not be interested in a testing solution using a scripting language such as Ruby. What a mistake!

Some might argue that the testing tool does look impressive. Wrong! We shall always select the automation framework first, judge it without its tool(s). It is the framework that decides the test script and its testing capability, while a good tool enhances the team's productivity. If the framework underneath a tool is not stable or lacking features, however impressive the tool may seem to be, it simply does not matter.

Expensive lesson for "looks like a good tool"

After attending my one-day Selenium WebDriver in-house training at one company, a tester told me this story. The project had one test automation attempt that failed within a week. The reason was the expensive testing tool (chosen by the test architect) did not support testing frames, which are used in the web app. As we know, failing to drive one step means being unable to test many scenarios. They contacted the support, got no help but frustrations.

Advice:

The choice is super easy. Go for the WebDriver standard, then you don't need to worry about

- feature completeness

- browser support (*all major browser vendors support and only support WebDriver*)

- execution stability

- performance

- documentation and technical support (*plenty of resources online*)

- cost (*free*)

- access to training

- seeking independent help from test automaton mentors

- integration with CT servers

- ...

Again, here are Microsoft's recommendations:

- Selenium WebDriver for testing web apps

- Appium + WinAppDriver for testing (Windows) Desktop apps

- Appium + iOS Driver/Android Driver for testing mobile apps

Wrong choice of test syntax framework

Behaviour Driven Development (BDD) has been a hot term in recent years, then BDD frameworks have been introduced to software testing. The idea of testing with BDD is not bad. However, BDD has been gradually misinterpreted as writing automated test scripts in a Gerkin-based syntax framework, such as Cucumber, SpecFlow and JBehave. This is wrong, very wrong.

The failures of test automation with Gherkin syntax often end with a big embarrassment. The idea was usually from a fake Agile Coach, and the management bought it. The painted picture sounds great: Business analysts can write "Given-When-Then" as executable specifications.

The reality is: too good to be true. To my knowledge, every test automation attempt using a Gherkin-based framework failed. The biggest failure I heard, *"The project spent 3 times of development efforts (measured time and money) trying to maintain those cucumber tests, eventually, dumped to the bin!"*

Why is Gherkin bad for test automation? The short answer is "hard to maintain". If you want to know more, you may refer to my other book "Practical Web Test Automation". Here I just show two quotes from the industry experts, one of them is the creator of Cucumber.

"Cucumber makes no sense to me unless you have clients reading the tests. Why would you build a test-specific parser for English?" - a tweet[1] by DHH (David Heinemeier Hansson), the creator of Ruby on Rails, cofounder & CTO at Basecamp and a best-selling author

"If all you need is a testing tool for driving a mouse and a keyboard, don't use Cucumber. There are other tools that are designed to do this with far less abstraction and typing overhead than Cucumber." - a blog post[2] by Aslak Hellesøy, the creator of Cucumber.

The below is a comparison of test tiers between a good test syntax framework RSpec and the bad Gherkin (when used for test automation).

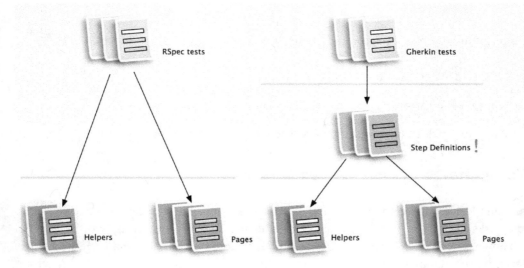

The extra effort (right graph) comes from the 'test-specific English parser', the part DHH was referring to. Cucumber is not the first failed syntax framework that using English-like syntax

---

[1]https://twitter.com/dhh/status/52807649145782272
[2]https://aslakhellesoy.com/post/11055981222/the-training-wheels-came-off

for automated testing (it may be for other uses, but definitely not real test automation). Do you still remember FitNesse (it was quite big about 10 years ago, an example here)? Now it is hardly mentioned.

Advice:

- RSpec

  It is simple, widely used (*190 million downloads for v3.8.0 alone*) and in scripting language syntax.

Wrong choice of test automation tool

First of all, we shall always "Choose Framework first, then tool". Otherwise, you (and your company) will be likely to be a victim of 'vendor-locking'.

Assume you have followed Microsoft's recommendation: using Selenium WebDriver (for webapps), and scripts are in a sensible script language. Your team still needs to use a tool to develop/debug test scripts efficiently. Generally speaking, two typical types of testing tools are:

- Programming IDE, such as RubyMine

- Code Editor, such as Visual Studio Code

Avoid Selenium IDE for serious scripts development

Selenium IDE[a], in my opinion, is badly named. It is in fact a record-n-playback tool with some extras. As Jason Huggins, the creator of the original Selenium, said in AAFTT Workshop 2009[b] "*Selenium IDE is the place to start with Selenium, but it is Selenium on training wheels*".

---

[a]https://www.selenium.dev/selenium-ide/
[b]https://craigsmith.id.au/2009/10/06/aaftt-workshop-2009-chicago/

Some readers probably have sensed that these are for writing code, not test scripts. Yes, these programming tools can be used for writing test scripts, but are not optimal. For example, I often saw engineers using a debugger to step over/into test scripts, which was very inefficient.

When you have a reasonable size of test suite running in CT, you simply are unable to keep up with test maintenance.

In 2007, The Agile Alliance held a workshop[3] to envision the next-generation of functional testing tools: "IDEs that facilitate things like: refactoring test elements, command completion, incremental syntax validation (based on the domain-specific test language), keyboard navigation into the supporting framework code, debugging, etc". According to the experts of this workshop, a next-generational functional testing tool is a dedicated testing IDE.

Here I won't go into the details of comparing programming IDEs and testing IDEs. Let me show you a couple of points on how an automated test engineer would like to do when debugging a functional test script:

- Leave browser open after test execution is finished, for inspection

- Run selected test steps against the current browser

As you can see, that's quite different from code debugging, right?

Advice:

- Use **TestWise** *(Disclaimer: I am the creator)*

  I started to design TestWise based on my testing needs back in 2006 and was happily surprised that TestWise's features were in line with 'The Next-Generational Functional Testing tools" defined by the Agile Alliance Workshop.

- Make your favourite programming IDE/editor work efficiently on developing/debugging test scripts

  Programming IDEs or editors (such as Visual Studio Code) has many plugins, it is worth spending time on finding good ones that will help to debug test scripts with high efficiency, trust me, you need it.

Test script in a compiled language

Many software teams use compiled languages (e.g. Java or C#) for scripting functional tests, which is wrong. We call test scripts for a good reason, i.e. test scripts shall be written in a scripting language, such as Ruby and Python. I am not saying it is impossible to implement high-quality automated functional testing in Java or C#, but it is going to a lot harder,

---

[3]https://www.infoq.com/news/2007/10/next-gen-functional-testing/

comparing to a good scripting language like Ruby. (*I have programmed Java professionally for over 10 years, and I published selenium books in both Java and C#*)

The common excuses for this mistake were absurd.

- "*Our application was developed In Java (or C#)*"

  But test scripts don't need to be in the same language as the target application uses. Test execution interacts with the application, its implementation language has nothing to do with functional testing (e.g. BlackBox testing). Between 2008 and 2012, Watir was widely used in large companies (including Facebook[4]) to test web apps written in all sorts of programming languages.

- "*We are a Java shop, we don't want to introduce another language*"

  Engineers who said this are often the ones who failed test automation (after significant investment from the company). Changes need to be made. Either 'try another approach, including a new framework in a new scripting language' or 'find a better way to implement in Java, learning from a good solution'. Over the years, I figured out this was just an excuse. When I presented the undeniable successful test automation solution (set up the core test on the first day and run regression tests daily), they used this excuse to do nothing.

Sadly, management tends to accept these wrong advice (using development language only for scripting auto functional tests) from technical architects who know little about test automation and CT.

Advice:

- Use wonderful Ruby language

  Medicare engineers tend to resist learning new things. If an engineer insisted on using his favourite compiled language (Java/C#/TypeScript) to write automated test **scripts** in a **scripting language**, is it possible that he can master test automation? I don't see it, as automated testing is much harder than development, a good mindset to embrace the change is mandatory.

- Do it in your preferred language well, prove in days.

  More meetings rarely help, pretty much in all industries. Test automation is objective and practical verification. If you cannot get a core end-2-end test scenario implemented within one day, game over, don't waste more time on it. The later work will be far more challenging such as:

---

[4]http://watir.com/facebook-watir-and-testing/

- training engineers (including manual testers) to master it
- maintain test scripts efficiently to keep up to date with application changes
- reliable test execution in CT (run many times a day)

Unreliable individual test execution

Many automation testers lack the concept of test execution reliability.

"7 out of 10 executions OK, the test pass!"

Once I was shocked by one tester performing the execution of automated tests. He would execute a test script 10 times, if it passed 7 times, execution of this test script was considered successful. Amazingly, this was accepted by the tech lead.

The reliability of automated test execution in CT requires much higher.

"What is your chance of green build, for average 90% pass rate?"

In a recent project, I was invited by another team to a discussion of implementing CT. I asked a senior test automation engineer: "*what is your tests' average pass rate?*". Seeing the confusing look on his face, I clarified: "*Averagely speaking, assuming test scripts are correct, if run one of your tests 100 times, how many passes?*". After a pause, he replied: "*About 90*". Then I said, "*You shall improve it to at least 98%, otherwise it pointless to pursue CT*".

This is just simple math. The probability of a green build for a suite of 75 tests with an average 90% pass rate is **0.04%** (*0.9 x 0.9 x 0.9 ... x 0.9*).

Continuous Testing with auto-retry can rescue unstable test execution to some degree. However, if the average test executive reliability is low (under 99%), this will be a waste of time to execute these tests in a CT server (even with auto-retry), as you will spend a lot of time dealing with many test failures (from frequent builds).

The wise approach is to review your test design and make the test execution reliable.

Advice:

- Improve infrastructure reliability if it is a part of the problem

- If the unreliability is only limited to a handful of test scripts, exclude them from CT, they are simply are not ready.

- For the potential issues in test frameworks/designs/scripts, seek help from a competent test automation coach.

Test scripts are poorly designed and hard to maintain

Well-designed test scripts are easier to maintain. When running a suite of automated tests regularly in CT, the impacts of poorly designed test scripts are greatly magnified. A habit of a good test automation engineer is that he sees an imperfect test script, he will refactor (please note, refactoring, not changing) it immediately. Maintainable test design is the core topic of my other book "Practical Web Test Automation", check it out.

Advice:

- Use Page Object Pattern

  There is quite a lot of information on this testing design pattern, which is considered as a Selenium's best practice[5].

Inefficient to debug test failures

The work of scripting one automated test is not complete after it passed, far from that. The major benefits of test automation shine mostly in regression testing. With CT, automated tests got run often, as a result, you will see many test failures.

Maintaining automated regression tests is not easy, for every CT build, the scope for test automation engineers is all user stories. For readers who are familiar with SCRUM, that is the work of all sprints. Once the team is getting used to CT, many activities such as deployments are dependent on it. The pressure for test automation engineers is high. Furthermore, if a test automation team does a good job, the quick feedback will provide confidence to check in more code changes. In other words, the better job you do, the more work you get.

Debugging failed tests (a large percentage of them may be false alarms) with high efficiency is the weapon to win continuous test maintenance battles.

Advice:

- Use a dedicated testing tool such TestWise

---

[5]https://www.selenium.dev/documentation/en/guidelines_and_recommendations/page_object_models

15.2 Failure Factors - infrastructure

Frequent end-to-end test executions, triggered in CT, rely on the supporting infrastructure. Because successful test automation is rare, many organizations do not realize the load generated by automated test execution, thus, lack investments in the high-demanding infrastructure. On the other hand, CT is more likely to fail, due to the insufficient (in both quality and quantity) infrastructure.

Lack of dedicated server infrastructure

Test automation shall have its own dedicated server environments. However, in most organisations, there are only one or two functional testing server environments (often called 'system test'), which are shared by manual testers, business analysts and test automation. Clearly, that is not ideal. The common problems are:

- Conflicted Test Data

  The data entered by different parties are more likely to cause conflicts. For example, a newly created user was deleted by others in the middle of test execution.

- Performance and reliability

  A resource-intensive operation, such as generating a report triggered by a manual tester, may cause automated test executions to fail.

Advice

- Set up multiple test server instances for test automation, exclusively.

WhenWise's 9 test servers

We set up 9 test server instances for testing WhenWise app, named ci1-whenwise, ci2-whenwise, ..., etc, exclusively for executing automated tests.

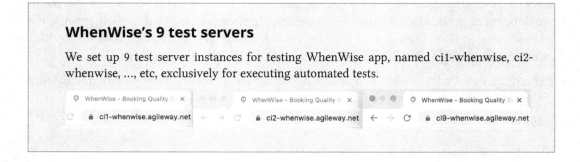

No dedicated test lab for automation

The test labs in the world's leading IT firms such as Facebook and Google have tens of thousands of machines. When I showed a picture of the Facebook test lab in my presentation, one audience said "that's because they have resources". Yes, that's correct. Money is an excuse for no setting up a test lab. Considering the two questions below.

- Is there a need?

  Clearly, Google and Facebook think so. But do you?

- If so, how many machines do you need for executing your current automation suite?

  The answer is usually not about money. Let's work out a sample case. Assuming a project has 50 Selenium tests, averagely 30 seconds execution time for a test. Therefore, the total execution time is 25 minutes.

  Now we set the target for 10-minute build time (an XP practice), 3 build agents are probably enough. You shall be able to set up a mini test lab: 1 server + 3 build agents on a laptop with 16GB RAM, using VM software. The total cost (including hardware + software) is about $2,000.

Advice

- Don't have to be Cloud-based, setup can be easy and very affordable

  Set up your own test lab using Virtual Box. In fact, according to a F8 conference presentation[6], Facebook's test lab in 2012 was just several Mac Minis on a rack.

Immature cloud-based deployment

Technically speaking, software deployment is not difficult. Having worked in the software industry for over 2 decades, I found that software teams were always able to push releases into production, while there were minor now-and-then deployment issues. An experienced programmer shall be quite comfortable on writing a script to package the software artifacts according to a certain format, such as Java's WAR file. For Ruby on Rails projects, there is no compiling and packaging required. I have worked on deployments (while I was a programmer) on many projects as a tiny side-work, which were hardly worth filling in a timesheet.

---

[6]https://www.youtube.com/watch?t=1896&v=X0VH78ye4yY

In recent years, I have seen many more issues with so-called container-based deployments. How could they make simple things harder? The answer is hype. One clear piece of evidence is a new job title: Cloud Engineer. There might be a need for dedicated cloud engineers in a large organization. For a small/medium company, it is unnecessary. Hiring them will most likely do more harm. Because they will make deployment architecture more complicated to justify their existence, naturally.

"We want CT, but can you help with container deployment first?"

In 2019, the CEO of a local IT company contacted me (via LinkedIn) for consulting on implementing Continuous Testing. He organized a conversation between his CIO and me to start. This CIO and I talked for about 15 minutes, then I realized that the CEO and the CIO have different understandings of the situation. The CEO wanted real Agile/DevOps, frequent releases. However, the biggest problem the CIO was facing was not testing at all. Their lengthy cloud-based deployment process (with many Docker containers) was so fragile that application errors occurred all the time. Test automation cannot fix their problem.

Advice

- Don't fall on false-hype of Docker/Kubernetes containers

  There will be always 'new' deployment technologies. Don't let the hypes fool you; Stay with the three key metrics of deployment: reliable, rapid and repeatable. If the deployment process with a new technology passes all the 3 metrics and is more efficient, use it by all means.

15.3 Failure Factors - continuous execution

Execution of automated functional tests is quite different from unit tests, the mindset and practices of executing unit tests in a traditional CI server will not work well for executing functional tests.

Long feedback

Some engineers and managers think running automated in a CT/CT server is like washing clothes in a washing machine. Throw clothes in, press the Start button and pick it up 45 minutes later. It sounds ridiculous, right? Have you heard of people saying this?: "Just kick off the build to run overnight". I did hear a lot, from those who have no idea of how test automation/CT works.

We know, compared to a unit test, the execution of an end-2-end UI test is much longer, in minutes. This matters. Let's say, the build time is 8 hours. After a piece of code checked in, a programmer unable to get feedback until tomorrow. He would continue working on other user stories or fixes. The next morning, the feedback came back, some regression issues were detected for that check-in. However, he has moved on. Here I just singled out one programmer with an easy-to-explain failed build, now considering a team of 10 programmers and many failed builds require investigations. My point is: short feedback time is critical in CT.

Quick assessment of 10-hour test automation solution: FAILED.

One manager (of a different division) once wanted to book a meeting with me to assess the status of test automation for a project. When she mentioned its execution in CI takes more than 10 hours, I told her, "the meeting is unnecessary, this solution has already failed." Long stories short, later, I saw the test scripts and its execution history in Jenkins. It was actually worse than I thought. For the two separate Jenkins build projects, the test pass rates were merely 17% and 44%.

A clear sign of a failed CT attempt is that growing execution time (with more tests), and the engineers have no clues to shorten it. They were hopelessly waiting, and kicked off another run with diminishing hope for a green build. To be fair, these engineers might be limited with the CI server (not CT server). Often, along with growing long execution time, the average test pass rates drop.

Advice:

- Parallel test execution

- Auto retry

- Inteiligne ordering

No Auto-retry and Manual-rerun

CT features such as Auto-retry and Manual-rerun greatly enhancement the build reliability. I pioneered (and implemented) the 'auto-retry' back in 2007 and have been using it ever since. With a medium-size regression UI test suite ($\sim$200 user story level tests), from my memory, 99% of successful builds utilise auto-retry. However, traditional CI servers do not come with Auto-retry for test executions.

Recently, I noticed 'auto-retry' feature in some 'new test frameworks', such as Jest and Cypress. It is wrong, as this complicates things unnecessarily, and it won't work well. If the target app server is busy, an immediate retry probably won't help. Plus, as a test automation engineer, I will feel embarrassed for writing the test scripts below (from Cypress documentation[7]).

```
it('allows user to login', {
  retries: {
    runMode: 2,
    openMode: 1
  }
}, () => {
  // ...
})
```

The bottom line is to leave the test script as it should be (focusing on test steps), let CT server handle retries.

It is possible to add Auto-retry support as a plugin to an open-source CI server such as Jenkins. I implemented one for CruiseControl back in 2007.

Advice:

- Implement auto-retry and manual-rerun

Prioritize test execution

It is common that inexperienced CT engineers break the automated tests into separated sub-suites when executed in a CI server. This is a form of 'test prioritization", the theory behind that is to execute high-priority test suites first and more frequently. It might sound logical to some, but it is very wrong and totally unnecessary.

---

[7]https://docs.cypress.io/guides/guides/test-retries.html#Custom-Configurations

- The effort for classification

  If prioritization is the way to go, some will be given to the job to set the priority for each test. As you can see there are efforts required and foreseeable disagreements.

- Missing tests

  The chances are some new tests will be forgotten to add to a suite, i.e., not run in CT.

- Confusion on status

  Let's say there are 3 test suites. If the high priority suite passed and the other two failed with a handful of failures, the test lead would classify a failed build. However, the manager or architect might argue this build is OK for a production release ...

- Low-priority tests will gradually be out of date

  Naturally, the lower-priority tests would get fewer runs in CT, and their failures will tend to be ignored by the team. Gradually, the test scripts became out of update with the app. There will be only one outcome: removing this low-priority suite from the CI process.

Advice:

- Run all tests in just one suite

Use conventional CI servers for CT

Conventional CI Servers such as Jenkins and Bamboo are built for executing unit tests, unless with special customisations, they are not suitable for executing automated UI tests. Over the last 14 years, I never saw a single successful UI test automation with Jenkins (and its previous name: Hudson). I am not belittling Jenkins or other CI servers, they were not designed for executing UI tests. Instead, repeated failed attempts of executing automated UI tests in CI servers is hurting their reputations.

CI Server (e.g. Jenkins)   UI Testing

Executing automated UI tests in a continuous process is an order of magnitude more difficult than executing unit tests.

	Unit Test	End-2-End UI test
Execution time	Fast, typically 0.1 seconds	Slow, typically in minutes
Reliability	Very reliable	Brittle
Effort to fix	Very low	High
Prone to changes	Very low	Very High

Having said that, it is possible to implement CT with CI servers with plug-ins that support the features I listed in the previous chapters, such as Auto-Retry, Intelligent Ordering, ..., etc.

The highest-pririty User Story: "Jenkins Must Die"

Once I joined a project which was told that test automation with CI in place. The test scripts were in Groovy and run in a Jenkins server. The test suite was split into 8 different Jenkins build projects. I was told the total execution time was over 12 hours. The build results were all over the place. The testing was mainly conducted by a manual tester. Running these automated tests in Jenkins was more just a getting a feel, such as *"80% of suite 1 pass, not bad"*.

I converted a few tests in raw Selenium WebDriver (Ruby), the manual tester found it was easy to understand. She learned it quickly. So we started to migrate the existing Groory test to Ruby and run them daily in a BuildWise CT server. The CI process (with Jenkins) has bothered the project manager (and the whole team) for quite a while. Seeing the vast difference, he created a user story card "Jenkins must die", and put it on the board, above all the cards. With more tests migrated over and run quickly in BuildWise, the regression testing cycle was greatly shortened.

> Shortly after I left the project, the manual tester (now an automated test engineer) sent me an email: "Killing Jenkins Today", as she migrated all tests over. In the email, she sent me a screenshot of the latest green build in BuildWise, completed 6 minutes with 10 build agents.

Advice:

- Switch to a proper CT server

- Implement CT features as plug-ins to the current CI server

15.4 Failure Factors - Human

"You think you can do these things, but you just can't, Nemo." - 'Finding Nemo' movie

Software development is a human activity, even more so for CT, as CT involves all members of a software team. Human beings make mistakes, especially on matters that they think they know but actually don't. Unfortunately, CT is that kind of matter.

Executives: like the idea, but not actively involved

Most of IT executives do not really understand CT (or Agile, or DevOps). From my conversations with a few CIOs, I could sense they have the desire to implement CT or test automation because a recent Gartner or Forrester report said so. That's why new test automation and CI/CD attempt often happens after a change of CIO.

Here are a few quotes I heard from some executives.

- "We spent 70% budget on (functional) testing, but releases are still buggy."

- "We cannot manually test the same stuff repeatedly. It does not make sense."

- "If there is no test automation, the work does not exist."

- "We shall not be afraid of pushing the releases more often, possible fortnightly. We will invest in test automation to make that happen."

In reality, the situation has not changed at these organisations. Functional testing was still conducted manually.

The reason: those executives like the idea of test automation and CT, but they are not actively involved. If an executive thinks a step further: what will change if CT is actually implemented? Just imagine you are equipped with Facebook's "release-twice-a-day capability" suddenly, will your teams still do these?

- 2-week sprint

- planning sessions that last hours

- various long meetings including story-point estimation sessions

- raise every defect in a defect tracking system

- care about 'velocity chart'

- ...

I doubt it, at least these activities won't be in the same way as before. Real CT means a fundamental change, as written in the Wired magazine's article 'The Software Revolution Behind LinkedIn's Gushing Profits[8]': "*completely overhauled its development and release process*".

The irony is that once an executive overcame the fear and decided to make it happen, CT will be the executive's 'best friend'. CT makes all software development issues transparent, otherwise, they would be easily hidden in various reports. The actions required by the executive is incredibly simple too, see below.

Advice:

- Visit all teams' regression test results on the CT server daily (let all staff be aware of that)

- Visit the teams regularly, ask them to show executing automated tests for a random feature

- Find (or lure) a good test automation & CT mentor, like what LinkedIn's CEO did

The hard part is to deal with the staff's fear of (and resistance to) changes. But that is a general leadership issue, isn't it?

---

[8]https://www.wired.com/2013/04/linkedin-software-revolution/

Tech leads/managers: pretend to know CI/CT

"It takes change to make change" - an Hooli Slogan in 'Silicon Valley' TV show

Despite many talking about CT, very few software engineers and managers have actually implemented (or witnessed) CT successfully for once. At the workplace, 'talking' skills win over 'technical' skills on most occasions, i.e. people with fancy titles such as 'test architect' and 'test automation lead' have to pretend they know. This unfortunate fact makes it even harder to implement CT properly. When a wrong person is in the position, most likely he will try to block any activities that will challenge his 'authority'.

I have met many of these 'test architects', many of them are quite nice people. If the middle managers and tech leads did not sense the passion and real actions from the executives (to make CT happen). Their default position is to delay doing anything seriously based on the past attempts on test automation or CT, which all had failed.

"You are not allowed to do test automation"

Many years ago, a test manager at a government department attended my presentation. He was very impressed, and engaged met in a short-term contract to work in his team as a senior test automation engineer. He was supportive at first , but it did not take long before the situation changed.

The testers in the team were using JMeter to invoke XML/HTTP services and verify the response manually. You heard me right, JMeter, a load testing tool. The reason for using JMeter was to enable them to select a JKS certificate for authentication. Apparently, it was inefficient. During that time, this test manager was trying to create a 'new' manual testing process based on the new ISO testing standard. According to the test plan, a group of 8 testers was to perform this round of regression testing in 2 months. To the manager's surprise, the efficiency of executing automated test scripts far exceeded his expectations to an uncomfortable level. The final result was that the total regression testing time with automated test scripts is about 20 minutes. Yes, 20 minutes vs 2 months of 8 testers.

After spending about a week understanding the system (mainframe), I worked out a much more efficient way to execute API testing with Ruby script, and run them in a CT server. I completed my share of testing tasks quickly, then helped the others. The efficiency of automated test execution was noticed beyond the test team. For instance, the developer lead came to me and ask: "how did you raise a dozen defects only within 10 minutes of a new build?". I showed him my test executions in a CT server. I think that upset the test manager, as it made his 'perfect test plan' obsolete.

Towards the end of my contract, the test manager wanted me to work on a new testing task at a different location. He got me in a meeting and asked me not to do automated testing. I rejected the request by saying "test automation is in my job description that you created. If I did not have the capability to do it, that's OK. However, at least I should have a try first". He insisted on no test automation. I did not renew the contract.

Advice:

- It is OK to acknowledge "I don't know test automation and CT"

  According to this article *5 Reasons Enterprise Test Automation Is So Challenging*[9], based on research Tricentis conducted from 2015 to 2018, *on Global 2000 enterprises, a dismal 8% have end-to-end functional tests running on a regular basis.* Please note, this is just "running regularly". It is far from comprehensive, or high-pass rate, or run multiple times a day, or if-pass-all-deploy-to-production. It would be safe to say, only < 10% out of that 8% can achieve the goal.

Tech leads: Fixated on a particular technology

"It doesn't make sense to hire smart people and tell them what to do; we hire smart people so they can tell us what to do." - Steve Jobs

A large percentage of test automation and CT attempts failed for this reason. Even some tech leads admitted that they are lack of knowledge of both test automation and CT (*which is respectable*), they tend to fixate on a certain technology or an approach without any supporting base, such as:

- The test script has to be in Java

- BDD with Cucumber tests

- Must use Jenkins to run UI tests

- Use SoapUI for API testing

- …

---

[9]https://www.stickyminds.com/article/5-reasons-enterprise-test-automation-so-challenging

One important characteristic of Test automation and CT is objectiveness. Why not putting the belief (along with alternatives) into testing and assess objectively? After all, we are talking about testing.

"Your Ruby solution is good, but we still want you to implement in Java"

During my consultation, I always was able to implement a key test case and set up running it in BuildWise on the first day, if the environment is ready. For one POC (proof of concept), I was given 3 months to implement 10 regression tests, converting from a failed Java solution. I completed the task in 3 days and all tests got executed reliably in BuildWise daily. In the report, along with the test scripts and execution stats (available live on the CT server), I explained some techniques/tools I used and the benefits of using raw Selenium WebDriver in Ruby.

The two tech leads were surprised at my work. The next day, their manager told me: "*we still want you to implement in Java*".

Advice:

- Change to a learning attitude

  Learning test automation and Ruby (from Jon Tirsen, my agile coach) are the two best things that ever happened to my IT career.

Developers: delay fixing regression errors

In Chapter 6, I stated that one criterion of a successful CT process is that developers stop and fix regression errors detected on CT. Every software engineer knows: for bug fixes, earlier is better, and cheaper too. However, from my observations, when I presented the regression errors minutes after code check-ins, except a small percentage of developers (*usually the good ones*), most developers showed no willingness to work on the fixes immediately. A common excuse is: "Cool, I will address them at the end of the sprint."

There are many negative impacts when developers delay fixing the regression errors:

- For every failed build, a passionate CT engineer will verify all test failures.

  As you can imagine, this is a lot of work. It is not reasonable to ask the CT engineers to ignore the failures in Test X and Test Y, but keep looking out for others. This would be absurd, as the main purpose of CT is to provide feedback quickly, which is considered highly-valuable in the world's top IT firms. The programmer's excuse is very wrong, the best time to fix a regression error is now, as the likely cause was the most recent check-in.

- A new regression issue may lead to a wrong development path

  If that is the case, all further development efforts will be wasted.

The fundamental reason for this is a failure of leadership. Here are some of the programmers' concerns:

- I don't like interruptions, I already started working on my assigned user story

- My time spending on fix regression errors does not help my workload for this sprint

- A regression issue could be someone else's fault

- My fix to a regression error may cause another regression issue

It is the manager's responsibility to address the above concerns and get the priorities right for the team.

Advice:

- No more code check-ins for new features on failed CT build

  Sound crazy? No, it actually worked very well for all my personal projects and some of my clients. Refer to the section '*Toyota Production System*' in Kent Beck's famous book: *Extreme Programming Explained: Embrace Change*.

Manual testers: fear of losing the job

> "*In software development, you can never test enough*" - Zhimin Zhan

By working closely with manual testers, I could sense their fear of test automation. This is easy to understand, as in many industries, automation (e.g. robots) replaces and reduces human jobs. However, the software industry is different.

As more software projects have adopted Agile methodologies (from Waterfall), the percentage of manual testers in a software team increased gradually, especially in large organisations. In the last two projects I worked on, more than 60% of team members were manual testers.

- Much more testing efforts with 'short release cycles'

  In theory, every Scrum project shall have a production-ready build for each sprint, typically in two weeks. That is a lot more testing effort than that of a 6-month release Waterfall project.

- More frequent releases mean more changes, i.e, more regression testing

  With frequent releases, the team will get more feedback from the customers. More feedback leads to more application changes requested, i.e, more frequent releases. As the software is in use, regression testing is essential, as a result, more testing efforts are required.

Most people will agree that with the above observations. However, some might think that this is the argument for test automation, which are the worries. The reason that the automation-replacing-manual-test did not happen yet, was because test automation failed in most software companies. Well, that's true. However, even at a project with a good CT process, manual testing is still required, but in a more efficient form.

- Exploratory Testing

  I am sure you have heard of 'Exploratory Testing', a type of software testing where test cases are not created in advance but testers check the system on the fly. No more boring test design in Excel, this is good news for manual testers.

  Thanks to test automation, manual testers are much happier at work. They now don't need to spend a lot of time on repetitive tasks. Instead, they can focus on high-quality manual testing.

- Help design automated test scripts

  Automated test script is just another form of conduct functional testing, the design of test steps and finding test data are not much different from manual testing.

- Help verify test failures

  When there are test failures in CT builds, which will happen often, someone needs to verify that manually.

My point is that the cake is big enough for all, so no need to fear. If you are a manual tester, why not learn test automation which will surely help your career. In fact, I received many thank-you emails from the manual testers I have mentored. Many of them had new job titles now: Software Engineer in Test, test automation engineer, team leader and even Scrum master. Some of them no longer work in test automation, but the experience boosted their confidence and understand software development better.

> ### Rocky's promotion
>
> Once I worked with a tester nicknamed Rocky who was in his fifties. Despite many doubts, he fell in love with automated testing quickly. His main doubt, which I knew later, was the fear of losing his job to automated testing. About 1 year after I left the project, I met Gary, another tester in Rocky's team. Gary said to me: "Rocky lost his job", I was shocked. Then he added slowly: "he got promoted".

Advice:

- Encourage testers to learn test automation

Agile coaches: Fake agile ceremonies

"No, this (too much ceremony) is wrong. I don't know what to do about it." - Kent Beck
('Father of Agile') in Being Human Podcast #23[10] (2018-08-31)

Many software projects overemphasized 'agile ceremonies' such as "Burn Chart", "Velocity", "Story Estimation" and "Retrospectives". As a result, their software development was jeopardized. I am not against the individual concepts, but the reality is that a number of 'agile consultants' has distorted the true meaning of Agile with these religious-alike processes.

Take Retrospective as an example, on most of the Retrospective sessions I have seen, managers were busy recording team members' notes (under "what went well" and "what needs improvement") and stored them into a digital form (such as a Confluence page). Then the job was done. A 9-year-old kid can master this within an hour and do similar things for reviewing a school activity.

Let me give you a more concrete example. I worked on a few fake or semi-fake agile projects as a tester, on retrospective sessions, I often raised the exact same item under "what needs improvement" column: Developer stop and fix regression test failures. (My automated test scripts, running in CI, can detect regression errors quickly on a daily basis. However, the developers often failed to act quickly.) While most of the team agreed and some project managers promised actions, up to date, the improvement never happened on those projects.

If the talking culture such as fake agile ceremonies dominates a software project, the real agile practice such as CT surely won't succeed.

---

[10]https://www.firsthuman.com/podcast/23-leaving-facebook-with-kent-beck/

Advice:

- Switch the focus from agile ceremonies to real Agile: test automation and CT

  Not everyone likes to do fake stuff. I have met some 'fake agile coaches' who wanted to do the real Agile, but were unable to, due to lacking the foundation: test automation and CT. It is a failure of leadership, rather than a failure of individuals.

Managers: The team spent too much time on JIRA, not CT

"It does not make sense that a software team spent more time on JIRA than working on their own software!" - Zhimin Zhan

In recent years, a new role has been added to software project teams: Agile Coach. Unfortunately, most of them are fake agile coaches who are not hands-on working on CT daily. They may severely hinder your project development.

Here are some typical activities that a fake agile coach will do:

- coordinate stand-up meeting, and get all team members to talk about their progress on assigned user stories in a JIRA Sprint Board

- write 'guidelines' on Confluence

- advice on how to arrange story cards on the wall

- have meetings with managers to 'assess/plan/predict' future development based on the current Burn Chart in JIRA

- get programmers/testers to estimate story points, sometimes even use ridiculous 'planning poker cards'

- create/drag story cards in JIRA to do 'sprint planning'

- run a retrospective session, record them in Confluence, the end (*no actions*).

- ...

"Maintain only the code and the tests as permanent artifacts. Generate other documents from the code and tests. Rely on social mechanisms to keep alive import history of the project. ..., Everything else is waste." - Kent Beck (Extreme Programming Explained 2nd edition, p. 66)

Based on my understanding of Kent Beck (the father of Agile)'s book and my personal experiences over the last 20 years, I think the above activities performed by an agile coach are a total waste of time. Worse still, fake agile coaches usually cause setbacks. They have to appear doing something. This 'the something' is usually wrong, such as adding unnecessary procedures Kent is referring to.

The biggest harm is that fake agile coaches tend to prevent real useful practices such as Test Automation and CT. Fake agile coaches fear CT, not because they understand what is good or bad, it is because CT interrupts their 'plans' and redirects the team back to what really matters: the software they are working on, not Atlassian's software. This will make their positions redundant.

The feedback of CT is real, it will guide the team to work and communicate better.

Still failed after switching JIRA to Rally

Once I worked in a large IT firm that was undergoing a 5-year agile transformation plan led by a chief "agile coach". She organized weekly Agile training sessions for a whole year, talking about the importance of story walls and estimation of story points, the usual fake agile stuff.

The time passed quickly, maybe after one year into the 5-year plan, there were no signs of improvements in software development (except more agile coaches roles added). Somehow, she managed to convince the CIO that JIRA was the problem, and recommended that Rally (another project management tool by CA) would work well. Hence, several months of work of all projects migrating the stuff in JIRA to Rally, under the 'guidance' of agile coaches. Not surprisingly, there were a lot of complaints. Personally, I rarely used either JIRA or Rally. My subjective view is that JIRA is better, my objective view is to avoid both, and focus on CT instead.

Anyway, as you can imagine, the agile transformation in this company was a mess. I decided not to renew my contract. About one year later, this firm was acquired by a competitor.

Advice:

- Dump JIRA (or equivalent), get back to the classic physical user story cards

  New-to-agile people think user stories in a digital form is normal. The reality is actually the opposite. "User story card" was called for three good reasons:

1. **User**, a business feature that can be verified (by automated tests)

   Ideally, every business feature shall be tested, in Agile, by automated test scripts.

2. **Story**, informal and concise

   The purpose of using story cards is to initiate conversations.

3. **Card**, on a physical card

Once a user story is done, implemented and captured in automated tests, the user story card will be torn off.

Managers: Not allocating time for on-going maintenance

Incompetent IT managers think that the work of software development is not much different from laying bricks for a wall. They like predictability. They believe more workers, the faster the job gets done. In those project manager's mind, the software engineers are fully replaceable. This is wrong, of course, as the classic "The mythical man-month" book explained it well. Unfortunately, quite a lot of software managers simply cannot get over that mindset.

This mindset makes it hard to implement test automation. Why? Most of the test automation efforts are spent on maintenance. Even more so for CT. How do you assign a story point of CT work? You can't, CT is supposed to an on-going activity. Moreover, the feedback of CT interrupts PM's plans. Now you can see why fake Agile coaches and some managers talked about test automation (*as the cornerstone of Agile*), but actually did little. Test automation and CT make them uncomfortable: these work are not reflected on the velocity charts.

The irony is, with real CT, the software releases are totally predictable. For all my apps, I release to the production the next day if there are changes or new features. If a feature is too big (or not clear), I implemented a part of it. My customers always get to try out the new features on the next day and provide me with quick feedback. It is more natural this way.

Advice:

- Executives forbid teams from using velocity charts as the progress indicators

  Make CT the most important activity in software development.

Executives/managers: CT engineers' hard work often is underappreciated

"*Testing is Harder than Development, If you want to have good testing you need to put your best people in testing.*" - Gerald Weinberg, in Podcast 'Testing is Harder than

Development[11]'

"In my experience great developers do not always make great testers, but great testers (who also have strong design skills) can make great developers. ..., A great 'career' tester with the testing gene and the right attitude will always be able to find a job. They are gold." - Patrick Copeland, Google Senior Engineering Director Copeland 10-2[12]

Continuous Testing is a prevention type of work. If a job is done well, few people will notice. If there are issues detected on CT, the team's focus will be on fixing the issues. Once the issues are fixed, most of the credits go to the developers.

Some manual testers take pride in the number of defects they have raised, referring to the records in the defect tracking system. However, for CT engineers, most of the issues are regression errors. CT engineers usually don't have time (no need anyway for repeated regression failures) to raise defects. In other words, the work of CT engineers will be easily forgotten due to lacking records.

The work of the automation and CT engineers (quite often, the same person) is hard, much harder than programmers. I am sure you have heard that some programmers complained about the interruptions. They reject tasks because they want to focus on the current user story. But for CT engineers, interruptions are a part of their daily work. For every CT run, they need to address testing failures for all user stories, please note, from all sprints. Moreover, the better job they do, the quicker feedback to the team. As a result, more work is going to come.

That's why in the world's top IT firms, CT engineers (with test automation) are called the best of the best. Sadly, this view is not shared by most software companies.

Advice:

- Pay (real) CT engineers well. More importantly, treat them with high respect.

  Otherwise, you will lose the good ones. The good ones, according to Google's Patrick Copeland, "are gold". A wise executive knows the importance of keeping its star staff, for IT, CT engineers top the list.

Executives/managers: wrong hirings

"95% of the time, 95% of test engineers will write bad GUI automation just because it's a very difficult thing to do correctly." - Alan Page, in Podcast 'Testing Lessons Learned at

---

[11]https://testguild.com/tribute-gerald-weienberg/
[12]https://blog.utest.com/2010/02/23/testing-the-limits-with-patrick-copeland-part-ii/

Microsoft with Alan Page[13]'

Test Automation and CT are rarely implemented at large IT firms (see the references earlier). The chances that you can just hire one good test automation or CT engineer are extremely slim. So don't count on it.

Funny quotes from fake test automation engininerrs

- *"Oh, I don't need double quotes for URL in Java"* - a newly hired test automation engineer
  When I pointed out the obvious missing quotes for URL in the first RSpec test she wrote: `"driver.get(http://a.site)"`

- *"What is Xpath?"* - a senior test automation engineer, claimed several years of experience in Selenium

- *"Regular expression, I know this. It is only for Ruby"* - a software engineer in test
  When I explained test scripts to him.

- *"Between Zhimin and I, we created these automated tests"* - a tester claimed to have done 20,000 RFT automated tests in the interview, but did zero after he was on board.

If the wrongly hired people are doing nothing, that's a good outcome. However, more often than not, they will sabotage the project. After seeing fake test automation at most projects, those people claimed "years of experiences in test automation and CI/CD" for a better-paid job and still hope to continue to do manual testing. As CT makes test automation real, this panics them.

A common tactic of those fake test automation engineers is to suggest an alternative test framework or tool. They made up lies about little/no maintenance work required with that tool, and how great it worked in their last project, ..., etc. For managers who had fixations on a perfect delivery plan based on a chart, they might buy it after seeing a well-presented demo video.

"The first piece of advice I give people when they ask for the keys to our success: Don't hire too many testers." - "How Google Tests Software" book, page 4. [Whittaker 12]

---

[13]https://testguild.com/alan-page-principles-lessons-learned-at-microsoft/

Advice:

- Find a good mentor who can deliver visible results in days

  If you are lucky to find one, do follow their advice.

- Hire new graduates and train your manual testers

  Under a good mentor, learning proper test automation such as Selenium WebDriver can be very fast.

16. CT with web app testing in other frameworks

So far I have been focusing on web test automation with Selenium WebDriver (*automation/-driver framework*) in RSpec (*syntax framework*). In this chapter, I will cover how to set up CT with Selenium WebDriver in other frameworks:

- PyTest (Python)

- Mocha (JavaScript)

- Cucumber (Ruby)

Astute readers will notice these frameworks (plus RSpec) are all in scripting languages. That's correct, BuildWise does not support compiled languages such as Java and C#. This is not about whether BuildWise can or can't, it is me choosing not to. The reason is simple, I believe test scripts are better in a scripting language.

16.1 BuildWise supports multi-frameworks

You may use the same BuildWise server to run tests in different syntax frameworks.

Prerequisite

- **Git**

- **Browser drivers** (such as ChromeDriver for Chrome)

- **BuildWise Server** installed
  See Chapter 2 or view the screencasts on the book site.

- **Sample test project**
  We will reuse the *c:\work\agiletravel-ui-tests* project (see Chapter 2).

16.2 PyTest (Python)

Python, a popular and elegant programming language. As a matter of fact, Python is rated as the top programming language in 2017 and 2018 according to IEEE Interactive Ranking[1]. Many will say it is due to the hype of Machine Learning, I agree. As a scripting language, Python is well suited for writing automated test scripts. Python is one of the five languages that Selenium WebDriver officially supports. The growing popularity of Python will certainly more or less reflects in testing, for example, out of my five "Selenium WebDriver Recipes" books, the sales of the python book steadily increased in 2017 and excelled others in 2018.

Python test syntax frameworks

I will use *unittest*, the standard unit testing framework comes with the language.

unittest

The unittest test framework is python's xUnit style framework, it is sometimes referred to as "PyUnit". Here is a sample Selenium WebDriver tests written in unittest framework.

```python
import unittest
from selenium import webdriver

class FooBarTestCase(unittest.TestCase):

  @classmethod
  def setUpClass(cls):
    cls.driver = webdriver.Chrome()

  @classmethod
  def tearDownClass(cls):
    cls.driver.quit()

  def setUp(self):
    self.driver.get("http://travel.agileway.net")

  def tearDown(self):
    self.driver.find_element_by_link_text("Sign off").click()
```

---

[1]https://spectrum.ieee.org/static/interactive-the-top-programming-languages-2018

```
def test_first_case(self):
  self.assertEqual("Agile Travel", self.driver.title)
  self.driver.find_element_by_name("username").send_keys("agileway")
  # ...

def test_second_case(self):
  self.driver.find_element_by_id("register_link").click()
  # ...
  self.assertIn("Register", self.driver.find_element_by_tag_name("body").text)
```

The keywords `class`, `setUpClass`, `setUp` and `def test_xxx` define the structure of a test script file.

- **class FooBarTestCase(unittest.TestCase):**

  Test suite name for grouping related test cases.

- **setUpClass()** and **tearDownClass().**

  Optional test statements run before and after all test cases, typically starting a new browser window in `setupClass` and close it in `tearDownClass`.

- **setUp()** and **tearDown().**

  Optional test statements run before and after each test case.

- **def test_xxx(self):**

  Individual test cases.

- **Assertions**

  `assertEqual()` and `assertIn` are PyUnit's two assertion methods which are used to perform checks. More assert methods[2]

You will find more about unittest from its home page[3].

pytest

pytest[4] "*makes it easy to write small tests*". The feature I like most is that pytest supports running Python unittest-based tests out of the box, in a simpler and more flexible way.

To install pytest.

---

[2]https://docs.python.org/3/library/unittest.html#assert-methods
[3]https://docs.python.org/3/library/unittest.html
[4]https://github.com/pytest-dev/pytest

```
> pip3 install pytest
```

To run a unittest test script file.

```
> pytest my_spec.py
```

Preparation

Our goal is to execute automated tests in Continuous Testing server, that is, instead of running on tester/developer's machine, we can manage test executions a lot better and simpler, like a click of a button. But at first, we need to make sure the machine (where the CT server runs) has got all the software installed.

1. **Python 3**

   Make sure Python is added to PATH (default option).

2. **Install Selenium-WebDriver** and required testing packages

   PIP is the package manager for Python. PIP comes with Python installer, run the command below to upgrade to the latest PIP version.

   ```
   > python -m pip install --upgrade pip
   ```

   Install Selenium-WebDriver.

   ```
   > pip3 install selenium
   Collecting selenium
     Downloading selenium-3.141.0-py2.py3-none-any.whl (904kB)
       100% |##############################| 911kB 525kB/s
     Installing collected packages: selenium
     Collecting urllib3 (from selenium)
     Downloading urllib3-1.24-py2.py3-none-any.whl (117kB)
     Successfully installed selenium-3.141.0 urllib3-1.24
   ```

   Install modules that are required in your test scripts. *xmlrunner* is a unittest runner that saves test results to JUnit XML reports, *faker* generates test data.

   ```
   > pip3 install xmlrunner faker
   ```

3. **Prepare sample test project** and install required testing gems

We will reuse the *c:\work\agiletravel-ui-tests* project (see Chapter 2).
Start a command line window (Terminal or macOS/Linux), run the commands below to install the libraries to run the test scripts in this project.

```
cd agiletravel-ui-tests/selenium-webdriver-python-unittest
install-lib.cmd
```

4. **Verify test execution**

Run a sample Python unittest test.

```
pytest --junitxml=result.xml test/01_login_test.py
```

If you see test execution in a Chrome browser and a presence of `result.xml` file, yes, you are ready for Continuous Testing.

Sequential Build

1. Click "**New Project**" on BuildWise

2. Click "**Fill demo project**" dropdown (on the top right) and select "**unittest (Python)**"

3. Change "**Working Folder**" to *c:\work\agiletravel-ui-tests*

4. Click "**Create**" button

New project

Option 1. Loading from a working folder or Specify manually

Fill demo project ▼

Project name:	AgileTravel Quick Build Python Unittest
Identifier:	agiletravel-quick-build-python-unittest

(lower case and unique, e.g. clinicwise-ui-tes

RSpec
Mocha (Node.js)
Cucumber
unittest (Python)

Working folder: /Users/zhimin/work/projects/agiletravel-ui-tests

(Specify the SCM checked out project folder on the machine running BuildWise server, e.g. /home/you/work. BuildWise will try to use the working git's origin URL as the repository URL, can be changed later along with the project working folder under ~/.buildwise).

UI test folder: selenium-webdriver-python-unittest/test

*(where the UI tests are, relative to project root directory, eg. **spec** or **ui-tests/spec**)*

Test results folder: selenium-webdriver-python-unittest/reports

The directory (relative path) contains generated JUnit style test reports (TEST-XXX.xml), such as spec/reports or log. The output of test reports is set by Rakefile. This setting is for Quick Build only.

Rake task for UI or API Testing: -f selenium-webdriver-python-unittest/Rakefile ci:ui_tests:quick

UI test framework: unittest (Python) ⇕

*(The task executing long running UI/API tests, e.g. **ci:ui_tests:quick**. You may configure this later.)*

Create   Cancel

This will create the project *AgileTravel Quick Build Python Unittest* in BuildWise.

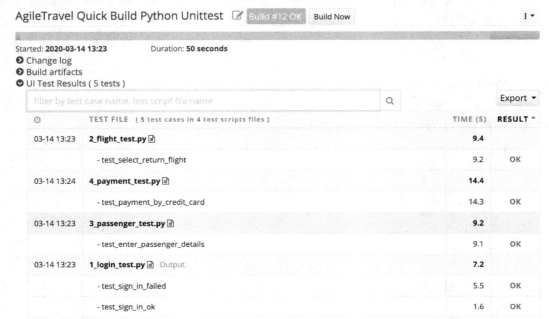

16.3 Mocha (JavaScript)

Over the years, JavaScript has evolved (such as Node.js and React.js) far beyond a client-side scripting language, and has become a powerful programming language that can also be used to create server-side applications, or even desktop applications (such as Microsoft's Visual Studio Code). JavaScript can also be used for automated testing, as a matter of fact, JavaScript is also one of Selenium's five officially supported languages.

One special note on JavaScript testing is its Asynchronous Testing. If you don't script correctly, test execution ends before its assertions get to run.

Mocha test syntax framework

In terms of the number of test syntax frameworks, JavaScript probably tops all the programming languages. From the purpose of CT, the syntax differences (among alls JS syntax frameworks) are trivial. BuildWise supports one JavaScript test syntax framework: **Mocha**.

Mocha is a popular Behavior-Driven Design (BDD) test framework for JavaScript (*Martin Fowler chose Mocha for his updated Refactoring book*). Here is a sample Selenium WebDriver tests written in Mocha.

```javascript
var webdriver = require('selenium-webdriver'),
                By = webdriver.By,
                until = webdriver.until;
var test = require('selenium-webdriver/testing'); // add 'test.' wrapper
var assert = require('assert');

var driver;
const timeOut = 10000;  // default to maximum timeout 10 seconds for one test case

test.describe('User Authentication', function () {

  test.before(function() {
    // run before all test cases, commonly initalize WebDriver
    this.timeout(timeOut);
    driver = new webdriver.Builder()
          .forBrowser('chrome')
          .build();
  });

  test.beforeEach(function() {
    // run before each test case, typically visit home page
    this.timeout(timeOut);
    driver.get("https://whenwise.agileway.net")
  });

  test.afterEach(function() {
    // run after each test case
  });

  test.after(function() {
    // run after all test cases, typicaly close browser
    driver.quit();
  });

  test.it('Test case description', function() {
    // one test case
    driver.getTitle().then( function(the_title){
      assert.equal("WhenWise - Booking Quality Services Near You", the_title);
    });
```

```
    driver.findElement(webdriver.By.id('partner-with-us-link')).click();
  });

  test.it('Another Test case description', function() {
    // another test case
  });

});
```

The keywords `test.describe`, `test.before`, `test.beforeEach` and `test.it` define the structure of a test script file.

- **`test.describe`**

  Test suite name for grouping related test cases.

- **`test.before()`** and **`test.after`**.

  Optional test statements run before and after all test cases, typically starting a new browser window in `setupClass` and close it in `tearDownClass`.

- **`test.beforeEach`** and **`test.afterEach`**.

  Optional test statements run before and after each test case.

- **`test.it`**

  Individual test cases.

I used Node.js' assert module[5] to perform checks: `assert.equal(...)`.

Preparation

1. **Node.js**

   Node.js 14.12 is the version used in this book's examples.

2. **Install Selenium-WebDriver** and required testing packages

   npm is the package manager for JavaScript. npm comes with Node.js installation.

   Install Selenium-WebDriver. Please note I used specific version `@3.6.0` here, this is because without it, the version installed will be a pre-release version `4.0.0-alpha.7` (at the time of writing), and it did not work well for me.

---

[5]https://nodejs.org/api/assert.html

```
> npm install -g selenium-webdriver@3.6.0
```

Conventionally, versions of required modules will be specified in `package.json` with the source.

Install modules that are required in your test scripts. *mocha-junit-reporter* is a mocha runner that saves test results to JUnit XML reports, *faker* generates test data.

```
> npm install -g mocha mocha-junit-reporter faker
```

3. **Prepare sample test project** and install required testing gems

Run the commands below to install the libraries to run the test scripts in this project.

```
cd agiletravel-ui-tests/selenium-webdriver-nodejs-mocha
install-lib.cmd
```

4. **Verify test execution**

Run a sample Mocha test.

```
mocha spec/01_login_spec.js --reporter mocha-junit-reporter \
   --reporter-options mochaFile=result.xml
```

If you see test execution in a Chrome browser and a presence of `result.xml` file, yes, you are ready for Continuous Testing.

Sequential Build

1. Click "**New Project**" on BuildWise

2. Click "**Fill demo project**" dropdown (on the top right) and select "**Mocha (Node.js)**"

3. Change "**Working Folder**" to *c:\work\agiletravel-ui-tests*

4. Click "**Create**" button

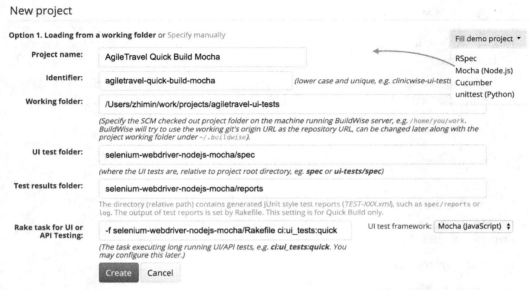

This will create the project *AgileTravel Quick Build Mocha* in BuildWise.

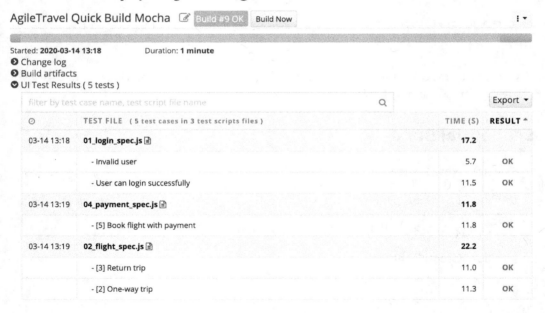

16.4 Cucumber (Ruby)

Cucumber is a tool for running automated acceptance tests written in a behaviour-driven development (BDD) style [Wikipedia]. Like RSpec, Cucumber is free, open-source and written in Ruby language. We have seen that tests in RSpec are quite readable, especially with the use of functions and page objects. Cucumber extends readability in tests even further with its plain text approach. Let's look at this sample cucumber test (also called feature):

```
Scenario: The user should be able to change their password
  Given I have a signed in user "agileway" with "testwise"
  When I am on the change password page
  And I fill in current password with "test"
  And I fill in new password and confirmation with "newpass"
  When I press "Update"
  Then I should see "Your password updated successfully"
```

However, the gain of improved readability comes with a huge maintenance cost for test scripts, as we now need another tier (called 'step definitions') to parse the syntax. For this reason, I don't use Cucumber (or its variants such as SpecFlow and JBehave) in my own projects. I have never seen a single successful project implemented functional testing with Cucumber-style syntax.

Preparation

1. **Prepare sample test project** and install required testing gems

   Start a command line window (terminal in macOS/Linux), and run the below commands to install the libraries to run the test scripts in this project.

   ```
   cd agiletravel-ui-tests/selenium-webdriver-cucumber
   install-lib.cmd
   ```

2. **Verify test execution**

   Run a cucumber test.

   ```
   cucumber --format  junit -o log/ features/01_login.feature
   ```

   If you see test execution in a Chrome (or other chosen) browser and the presence of log/TEST-features-01_login.xml file, yes, you are ready for Continuous Testing.

Sequential Build

1. Click **"New Project"** on BuildWise

2. Click **"Fill demo project"** dropdown (on the top right) and select **"Cucumber"**

3. Change **"Working Folder"** to *c:\work\agiletravel-ui-tests*

4. Click **"Create"** button

This will create the project *AgileTravel Quick Build Cucumber* in BuildWise.

AgileTravel Quick Build Cucumber ✏ Build #8 OK Build Now   ⋮ ▾

Started: **2020-03-14 13:15**   Duration: **57 seconds**
❯ Change log
❯ Build artifacts
◉ UI Test Results (5 tests)

| | | | Q | Export ▾ |

○	TEST FILE (5 test cases in 3 test scripts files)	TIME (S)	RESULT ▲
03-14 13:16	**04_payment.feature** 📄	**11.5**	
	- Passenger Details	11.5	OK
03-14 13:16	**02_flight.feature** 📄	**26.1**	
	- Oneway Trip	13.4	OK
	- Return Trip	12.7	OK
03-14 13:16	**01_login.feature** 📄	**5.6**	
	- Deny access due to invalid password	3.5	OK
	- Registered user can log in sucessfully	2.1	OK

16.5 Parallel Build with multi frameworks

BuildWise Agent supports Mocha, PyTest and Cucumber in the same way as RSpec, invoking the test scripts with a correct mechanism based on their file extensions. The below are sample parallel builds for PyTest, Mocha and Cucumber frameworks.

- PyTest (Python)

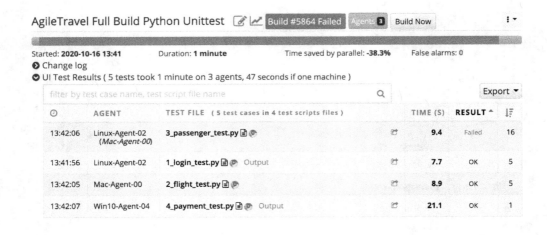

- Mocha (JS)

- Cucumber (Ruby)

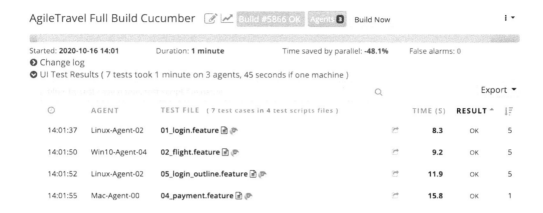

16.6 Review

In this chapter, we examined how to run Mocha, PyTest and Cucumber tests in BuildWise. As you can see, BuildWise manages executions of the tests in those frameworks no different from RSpec. You probably have noticed that, in Continuous Testing, the syntax framework, such as RSpec and Mocha, is the one matters, not the automation framework such as Selenium and Watir.

17. CT with Native apps and Microservices

So far, we have been doing CT with web apps. How about testing native apps or microservices in CT? The answer is "The same way". In this chapter, I will briefly show executing Appium and Non-UI functional tests in BuildWise.

17.1 Will my tests run in this CT server?

A typical automated functional test script uses two frameworks: automation and syntax. For example, Selenium WebDriver is an automation framework that drives a browser; RSpec is a syntax framework that defines the structure and provides assertions. As far as CT is concerned, the syntax framework is the one that matters.

BuildWise supports four syntax frameworks: RSpec, Mocha, PyTest and Cucumber. Test scripts in a syntax framework other than these four, such as JUnit, won't work in BuildWise. However, you may add the support for another syntax framework to BuildWise, as it is free and open-source.

To run test scripts in an automation framework such as Selenium WebDriver and Appium, just make sure the libraries are installed correctly on the CT server machine (for sequential builds) and the build agents (for parallel builds).

17.2 Desktop App Testing with Appium

Appium is an open-source automation tool for testing native applications on mobile devices and desktop apps. Here is an Appium (in RSpec) test script that drives the Calculator App on Windows (WinAppDriver is required).

```ruby
require 'rspec'
require 'appium_lib'

describe "Appium Windows Calculator" do

  it "Plus two numbers" do
    desired_caps = {
      caps: {
        platformName: 'Windows',
        deviceName:   'Surface Pro',
        app:          "Microsoft.WindowsCalculator_8wekyb3d8bbwe!App"
      }
    }
    driver = Appium::Driver.new(desired_caps, true).start_driver
    driver.find_element(:name, "One").click
    driver.find_element(:name, "Plus").click
    driver.find_element(:name, "Three").click
    driver.find_element(:name, "Equals").click
    the_dispaly_result = driver.find_element(:accessibility_id, "CalculatorResults").text
    expect(the_dispaly_result).to eq("Display is 4")
    driver.quit
  end

end
```

The setup of running Appium tests (as the above) in BuildWise is exactly the same as what we did for Selenium tests. The below is the screenshot of a successful parallel build (with 3 agents) of TestWise (a native app) on Windows 10.

TestWise Regression - Parallel ✏ 📈 Build #5944 OK Agents ❸

Started: **2020-11-07 06:16**   Duration: **47 minutes**   Time saved by parallel: **54.5%**   False alarms: 9
❯ Change log
⊙ UI Test Results (265 tests took 47 minutes on 3 agents, 1 hour 44 minutes if one machine)

	AGENT	TEST FILE (265 test cases in 170 test scripts files)	TIME (S)	RESULT ^	⬇
06:16:57	Win10-Agent-05	305_refactor_extract_function_shortcut_spec.rb 📄 ᗒ	**23.1**		28
		- Refactor - Extrract Function - Selenium Parameters Ruby - Shortcut Extract Function - using shortcut to apply refactoring, lower case Ruby/Python parameters	14.4	OK	
06:17:01	Win10-Agent-04 (*Win10-Agent-01*)	304_refactor_extract_function_normalize_param_spec.rb 📄 ᗒ	**24.5**		28
		- Refactor - Extrract Function - Selenium Parameters Ruby Extract Function - nomalize parameters	15.8	OK	

17.3 Non-UI Functional Testing

I prefer the term "Non-UI Functional Testing" over "Microservices testing". The latter one has some levels of hypes and abstractions, in my opinion. Non-UI functional testing is to test the business functions of an application without interacting with UI. SOAP/REST web service and Database testing fall into Non-UI functional testing category.

Non-UI functional testing characterists

Comparing to UI testing, Non-UI functional test execution is

- **faster**

- **more reliable**

Therefore, implementing CT with non-functional tests is easier. Most CT features covered in the previous chapters, such as Sequential/Parallel setup, Auto-retry and intelligent ordering, apply to non-UI test executions as well. The only exception is 'Capture error screenshot' as there is none.

```
describe "REST WebService" do

  it "Rest-Client: Get and Update" do
    require 'rest-client'
    require 'faker'
    response = RestClient.get "http://www.thomas-bayer.com/sqlrest/CUSTOMER/2"
    expect(response).to include("<ID>2</ID>")

    new_city = Faker::Address.city # randomly generated
    RestClient.post("http://www.thomas-bayer.com/sqlrest/CUSTOMER/2",
      "<CUSTOMER><CITY>#{new_city}</CITY></CUSTOMER>")
    get_response = RestClient.get "http://www.thomas-bayer.com/sqlrest/CUSTOMER/2"
    expect(get_response).to include(new_city)
  end

end
```

Use GUI tools such as SoapUI and Postman to assist test creation, but not for execution

Like automated UI test scripts, Non-UI test scripts shall use a scripting language. A common mistake is to use GUI tools such as SoapUI and Postman to develop and execute tests, for the following reasons:

- Lack of flexibility, due to vendor locking

- Impossible or difficult to integrate with CT

- Lack of synergy between non-UI and UI test scripts

Here is how I test SOAP web services:

1. Use SoapUI to generate a sample SOAP request XML

2. Convert the sample XML as an ERB template, with placeholders for injecting data

3. Develop test cases (using the template) in TestWise IDE

4. Run all tests in BuildWise, starting with a sequential build

5. Create a parallel build when the test execution time is long

The below is the screenshot of a failed sequential build on a BuildWise server (macOS).

API Testing Ruby Book Recipes ✏️ 📈 Build #5880 Failed

Started: **2020-10-23 08:57**   Duration: **1 minute**
❯ Change log
⊙ UI Test Results (67 tests)

	TEST FILE (67 test cases in 11 test scripts files)	TIME (S)	RESULT ^
10-23 08:57	**ch03_rest_spec.rb** 📄 Output	**10.1**	
	- REST - List all records	0.7	OK
	- REST - Get a record	0.7	OK
	- REST - Create a new record	0.7	OK
	- REST - Update a record	0.7	OK
	- JSON REST webservice using Rest-Client	0.9	Failure

18. Other Uses

Besides functional test execution, the set-up of CT has other uses as well.

18.1 Load Testing

Traditional HTTP-request-based load testing tools such as JMeter do not work well on modern dynamic apps. There is a trend to use a large number of 'real browser sessions' to perform real load testing. The parallel testing lab that you set up for functional testing can be used for load testing as well.

BuildWise supports executing Selenium WebDRiver scripts for load testing mode, in multiple build agents.

Execution Mode   ○ **Sequential** Functional Testing   ○ **Parallel** Functional Testing   • Parallel **Load Testing**

Here is how load test execution works in BuildWise.

1. Test scripts (selenium) were run on multiple build agents (same as parallel functional testing), except that test execution was repeated to generate maximum load.

2. The timings such as 'visit home page took 1.2 seconds' and 'login took 2 seconds' are sent to the CT server

3. CT server aggregates all the timings and transforms them into load testing metrics such as requests per second and average response time for an operation.

"An unexpected load testing solution"

On a consultation project, I did an internal demonstration of executing Selenium tests in BuildWise with 3 agents, on my laptop. The tech lead showed great interest. He told me that the No.1 tech challenge for the company is to generate a load of 5000 units (here I used the term *unit* to not reveal my client's business), the load testing team failed despite

working on it for over a year. Long story short, the mission was accomplished within one
week, using one BuildWise server with only 10 agents.

A load testing example

Below is a script to load testing the following operations.

- Visit home page

- Visit login page

- Sign in

- Sign out

```
load File.dirname(__FILE__) + "/../load_test_helper.rb"

describe "Load - Repeat Login" do
  include LoadTestHelper

  before(:all) do
    @driver = $driver = Selenium::WebDriver.for(browser_type, browser_options)
    log_time("Visit Home Page") { @driver.get(site_url) }
  end

  after(:all) do
    dump_timings
    @driver.quit unless debugging?
  end

  it "Sign in repeatly" do
    load_test_repeat.times do
      log_time("Visit Home Page") { visit("/") }
      log_time("Visit Login Page") { driver.find_element(:id, "sign-in-btn").click }
      driver.find_element(:id, "email").send_keys("james@client.com")
      driver.find_element(:id, "password").send_keys("test01")
      log_time("Sign in") {
        driver.find_element(:id, "login-btn").click
```

```
        driver.find_element(:id, "profile-dropdown") # verify user profile icon
      }
      log_time("Sign out") { visit("/sign-out") }
    end
  end
end
```

Some readers might figure out that this is a Selenium WebDriver script. Yes, you may 'preview' a load test script: viewing execution in a browser.

The setup and procedures of running a load test in BuildWise are exactly the same as it for parallel functional testing.

⊘ UI Test Results (7 tests took 3 minutes on 7 agents, 13 minutes if one machine)

⊘	AGENT	TEST FILE (7 test cases in 7 test scripts files)	TIME (S)	RESULT ⌃	⌷≡
12:38:17	Linux-Agent-06	load_repeat_login_spec.rb 📄 💬	**110.4**		6
		- Load - Repeat Login Sign in repeatly	106.7	OK	
12:38:18	Win10-Agent-04	load_repeat_login_spec.rb 📄 💬	**100.1**		6
		- Load - Repeat Login Sign in repeatly	92.2	OK	

In load testing mode, BuildWise will display the load metrics.

⊘ Load Test Results

VUs: **7**   Hits: **567**   Hits per second: **4.3** (Peak: **20.3**)   Errors: 0

Response times

Operation	#	Average (ms)	Fastest (ms)	Slowest (ms)	Error
Visit Home Page	147	1044	173	4687	
Visit Login Page	140	1036	148	9866	
Sign in	140	1686	650	3300	
Sign out	140	1008	182	2980	

and with charts.

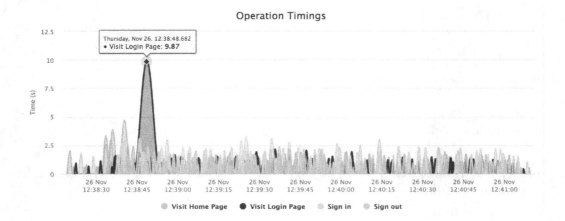

18.2 Cross-Browser Testing

Cross-browser testing with automation scripts has been overrated. The fact is that most projects are struggling with automated testing in just one browser type (Chrome), there is no point trying those failed scripts in Firefox, Safari and Edge. There are commercial providers for cloud-based cross-browser testing services (with Selenium), such as Sauce Labs and BrowserStack. The good news is that once you have CT implemented, you get cross-browser testing free, with little effort.

We have covered a bit about cross-browser testing in the previous chapters. Here is a quick recap. Design your test scripts to use an environment variable to set the browser type, like below:

```ruby
driver = Selenium::WebDriver.for(browser_type)
# ...
def browser_type
  if ENV["BROWSER"]
    ENV["BROWSER"].downcase.to_sym
  else
    "chrome".to_sym
  end
end
```

Then you can set the build project to run tests against different browsers.

Sequential Build

Set up multiple build projects with different browser settings.

Parallel Build

Set the browser type in the build agent's settings.

18.3 Prepare Application Data

The whole project team can enjoy the benefits of CT as the key process of DevOps. From my own experience, business analysts are often the first ones to realize the value of CT, earlier than the testers. During the development of a typical enterprise application, after a few sprints, business analysts found themselves spending more and more time on getting application data. Take an insurance claim app as an example, a business analyst may want the following data scenarios:

- a new application is created by a customer

- an application submitted for review

- a rejected application

- ...

For each scenario, it might take a business analyst a few minutes to navigate the app and fill in the information correctly. The repeated processes are not productive and could get quite frustrating. When a business analyst saw automated test execution on my computer, quite often, she asked me to help to generate some application data. So I did. Then another business analyst came, ..., etc.

To make it easier for business analysts, I usually create one or two build projects in BuildWise, so that they can help themselves to run the build and get their application data, anytime.

18.4 Requirement Traceability

"I have, in 30 years in the business, in industry, research and a little bit in government, NEVER seen a traceability matrix pays off." - Alistair Cockburn[1], co-author of "The Agile Manifesto"

Requirement Traceability is only valuable if it can be done quickly and dynamically. BuildWise supports an easy way to generate requirement (to functional test) traceability matrix, in seconds.

Understand Requirement Traceability first

Traceability (from the requirement) to code level is wrong. It is a complete waste of time in an agile project, in which code refactoring happens all the time. Hundreds of lines of code change may occur in seconds by using refactoring support in IDE. The only meaningful traceability is between requirements and functional tests, as a functional test verifies a user story (requirement) functionally.

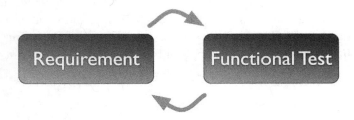

Enable requirement traceability in functional test scripts

The approach used in BuildWise is simple, just append user story IDs in the test case name, wrapped in a pair of '[' and ']'.

```
it "[12, 34] User can change password" do
```

---

[1]https://www.infoq.com/news/2008/06/agile-traceability-matrix/

Generate Requirement Traceability with ease in BuildWise

1. Navigate to a project setting page, click 'User Stories' button

2. Upload user stories CSV

A sample CSV is provided, in a very simple form. It shall be very easy to create the user stories CSV file (based on the sample) from export from JIRA.

3. Generate Requirement ↔ Test traceability

Click the 'Refresh Traceability Matrix' button, and click the 'Generate' button

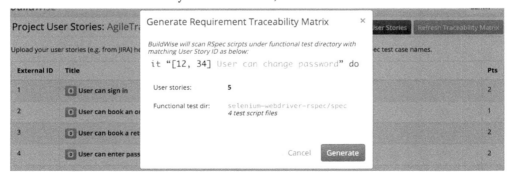

4. View traceability

The coverage (%) is shown at the top, and you may view the test script (content) associated with each user story.

5. Export Requirement Traceability Matrix

Click the 'Export Excel' button to export a traceability spreadsheet.

Requirement Traceability Matrix

Requirement test coverage:	**100%**
User Story count:	**5**
Test script files count:	**4**
Test case count:	**6**

Test Cases / Requirment IDs						
After generation, apply B11 fomula to the rest cells in row 11.	2	0	0	0	0	(
TC 1: [1] Can sign in OK	x					
TC 2: [1] User failed to sign in due to invalid password	x					
TC 3: [3] Return trip			x			
TC 4: [2] One-way trip		x				
TC 5: [4] Can enter passenger details (using page objects)				x		
TC 6: [5] Book flight with payment					x	

18.5 Execute specific tests on Server via Web Interface

A team member who has no test automation tool installed on his machine can still run an automated test via the CT server's web interface.

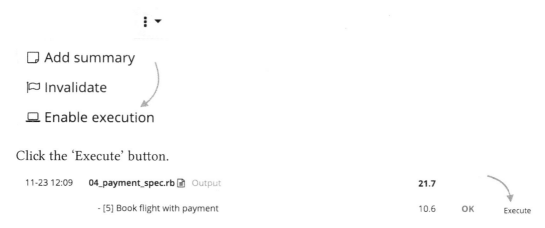

Click the 'Execute' button.

The output of the test execution (*clicking 'Output' link*) might be helpful.

18.6 Utilities

CT server is also a good place to offer the team some utilities. For example, querying the database for a certain data scenario is a common activity. Documenting the SQL in a Confluence page is not a good idea, as it may get outdated quickly. On recent projects, I created a 'utility build project' on BuildWise to offer some utilities, which were well received by the teams.

The process is similar to the above 'executing a specific test', except that the test script can take user-supplied inputs for custom execution. It is better to explain with an example. The test script below has two wildcard attributes A and B.

```
it "[US-06] Assert Failure", :wildcards => "A,B" do
  # BuildWise will pass user entered data as ENV['A'] and ENV['B']
  expect(ENV["A"].to_i + ENV["B"].to_i).to eq(-1)
end
```

A and B are the placeholders for user-entered input. You can set some pre-defined options for those wildcards in a `wildcard-config.json` file (*in the same folder as the test script*).

```
{
  "A": [],
  "B": ["1", "2"]
}
```

Here is a screenshot of custom test execution.

Execute test case with custom data   ✕

Test Case: **[US-06] Assert Failure**

A		=	-3
B		=	×2
			1
			2	0.333 s	Execute

```
Run options: include {:locations=>{"/tmp/sample-rspec-sequential/spec/03_assertion_spec.rb"=>[20]}}
.

Finished in 0.00107 seconds (files took 0.1332 seconds to load)
1 example, 0 failures
```

18.7 Wrap up

While some of the above CT server features might sound cool to some, please remember, those are only add-ons. Focus on the core CT process: executing automated End-2-End tests in a CT server regularly.

Appendix 1 CI Steps

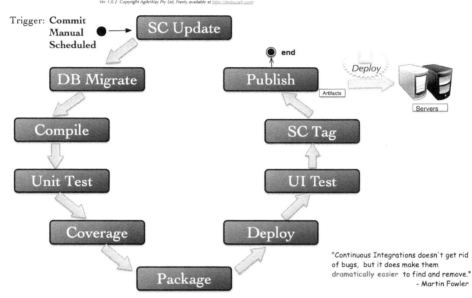

Continuous Integration In Nutshell

Ver 1.0.2 Copyright AgileWay Pty Ltd, freely available at http://testwell.com

Trigger: **Commit**
Manual
Scheduled → SC Update

DB Migrate

Compile

Unit Test

Coverage

Package

Deploy

UI Test

SC Tag

Publish

end

Deploy

Artifacts

Servers

"Continuous Integrations doesn't get rid
of bugs, but it does make them
dramatically easier to find and remove."
- Martin Fowler

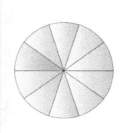

SC Update

Continuous Build, simply speaking, is building the software as long as new changes committed into the Source Control System. There are two ways:

1. A post-commit call back
2. More common way now-days for build servers poll the source control server, only start building where there are new commits.

If your SC is supported by the CI software, then usually you don't need to do anything for this step, except installing the source control command line (or called client) tools.

 Do not install SC UI tools (such as TortoiseSVN) on the Build Server, to avoid conflicts by manual SC operations

If your CI server supports scheduling, try schedule 2 builds daily
* lunch time
* after work

don't have source control, this is scary.

Difficulty Level:

Necessary:

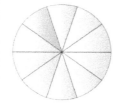

DB Migrate

During the life of software development, inevitably, your database schema needs changes along the development, and in fact, quite frequently. For example, creating a new table or adding a new table column. This is need to done systematically. If the database structure is matching code, there is no point to go further, that's why it is the first build step.

The database migration scripts do the two things (in sequence)
1. Identify the schema version of current database
2. Apply the changes after the

Also ability to revert back to a specific version is good.

Ruby on Rails has robust and easy-to-understand migration mechanism
- JRuby on Rails works too if you have to use Java platform

Avoid database diff tools

hack database changes through SQL UI tools

Difficulty Level:

Necessary:

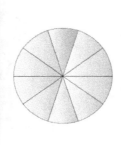

Compile

This only applies to compiled languages such as Java or C#. You don't need this step if using dynamic language such as Ruby.

As a part of a build process, code compiling shall be invoked from command line, not in IDE such as Visual Studio.

Generally compiler various options such as: with debug info, optimized, deprecated warnings, etc. It is ok to do compilation more than once, for example, one with unit test and code coverage containing instrument and debug info, the other for optimized release version.

* Always turn on compile warning flag, there are there for purposes.
* Develop a convention and good habits in setting classpaths used compilation build step

Difficulty Level:
⭐⭐⭐

Necessary:
⭐⭐⭐

Unit Test

I prefer calling it "Programmer Test", as it is one of most misused software terms in statements "tester A is assigned to unit test the user authentication module", which is black-box functional testing.

Unit test, as key concept of Test Driven Development, helps producing not only robust code, more importantly better designed code. If your code is hard to write unit test, its design is most likely not optimal.

Programmers who claims 'refactoring code' without suite of unit tests really is 'cow-boy change with hope for good luck'. No unit tests, not code refactoring.

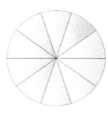

* The better your design, the easier to write unit tests
* Unit test database access with in-memory database
* Use Mock Objects
* Unit tests shall be very fast, try aiming < 0.1 second each averagely
* If your architects spent more time on whiteboards than unit tests, that's worrying sign.

Difficulty Level:

Necessary:

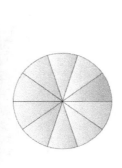

Coverage

Code coverage is measuring percentage of code (in terms methods/lines) covered by unit tests. This help find out untested and redundant code, keeping source code tidy and lean. Also it is a good insensitive for Test Driven Development.

In reality, achieving 100% code coverage is often not practical, 80% is already a good figure. At matter of fact, you may find many projects without code coverage data or at single digit percentage.

By including code coverage into build process, can help new/junior (not by age) programmers develop habits writing unit tests.

Code coverage tool modifies source code (called instrument) for collection coverage data. So remember to re-compile again for release version.

Difficulty Level:

Necessary:

Package

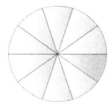

A typical software release contains not just source code, configurations, even web documents, file templates, ..., etc. This step is mostly concerned how to package files into a specific format, for example, a war file is zipped file format used for web applications developed in Java.

There are not much techniques to talk about here, however, people can still do badly. I have seen a project with very long packaging process: with hundreds of EJB jars!

If possible, try packaging your application into self-runnable in a zip file, so users can download the zip from CI artifacts, then unzip and run! This will not only impress your customers and have practical benefits!

Difficulty Level:

Necessary:

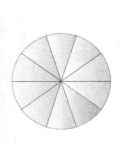

Deploy

Depending on the nature of your application, deployment can be quite complex (many heavyweight frameworks) or very simple (such as Ruby on Rails). Commonly, deployment process consists of the following steps:

1. stop the server if it is currently running

2. unpack the new release

3. update database schema (database migration)

4. update configuration

5. start the server

Try make all above into a single command, which can be easily invoked by the CI server.

Unit test database access with in-memory database detect eary

Difficulty Level:

Necessary:

UI Test

This step is, unfortunately, often ignored by projects, because they cannot implement the maintainable automated UI test scripts. If doing it wisely, it can be done and it is not that difficult.

UI test execution is going to be slow (comparing to unit tests) due to its nature. Try breaking UI tests into two groups:

* Quick Build: a handful of key UI tests
* Full Build: all UI tests

For full build, distribute them into multiple build agents to execute in parallel, further shorten feedback loop by injecting failed test cases from Full Build into Quick Build.

For long Full Build, implement build agents in a plug-in-run way, i.e., new build agents can be added to contribute any time during the build; existing build agent can pull out without much impact.

Display the test result as soon as a test case execution is complete

Intelligent ordering, run error-prone or new tests first.

Display the error trace for failed test and show the test script on CI web interface. Even better, users can click the test case name on CI web page to open it in their testing IDE.

Difficulty Level:
☆ ☆ ☆ ☆

Necessary:
☆ ☆ ☆

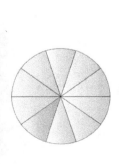

SC Tag

Tagging refers to labelling the repository at a certain point in time so that it can be easily retrieved in the future, this is to achieves repeatable builds. It is generally very easy to do so, for example, in Git

git tag v1.2.2

You don't have to label every build, probably only for successful ones, especially full builds passing all tests. Be ware of the time difference between checking out from source control and actual tagging. A common approach is to introduce 'Code Freeze' or schedule full builds at night time.

It is a good idea have tagging (and branching) conventions, I like the one used in GitHub,

Branches:
    master
    1-2-stable

Tags:
    v1.2.3
    v1.2.4

Difficulty Level:

Necessary:

Publish

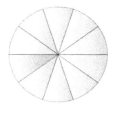

Once a build finishes, there are numerous ways to publish the result to the team. One common way is Email, and of course with the status showing on the CI server.

Apart from the success/failure indicator, build results might also highlighted failed test cases and artifacts (files generated out of the build process). Some CI servers might keep the build history, which can be generated into pretty graphs for reporting purposes.

Once a CI process is mature, the CI is the 'heart' of the team, so aim for direct, simple, and concise if possible.

Lava Lamp is a good option as the slow, smooth movement lava might help reduce some stress levels.

Difficulty Level:
☆☆☆☆☆

Necessary:
☆☆☆☆☆

Resources

Scripts

http://zhimin.com/books/practical-continuous-testing[2]

Username: `agileway`
Password: `BUILDWISE20`

Log in with the above, or scan QR Code to access directly.

Books

- **Practical Web Test Automation**[3] by Zhimin Zhan

  Solving individual selenium challenges (what this book is for) is far from achieving test automation success. *Practical Web Test Automation* is the book to guide you to the test automation success, topics include:

  - Developing easy to read and maintain Selenium WebDriver tests using next-generation functional testing tool
  - Maintainable Test Design with Reusable Functions and Page object model
  - Functional Testing Refactorings
  - Strategies on team collaboration and test automation adoption in projects and organizations

- **Selenium WebDriver Recipes in Ruby**[4] by Zhimin Zhan

  The problem-solving guide to Selenium WebDriver with over 150 ready to run recipe test scripts.

- **API Testing Recipes in Ruby**[5] by Zhimin Zhan

  The problem-solving guide to testing API such as SOAP and REST web services.

---

[2]http://zhimin.com/books/practical-continuous-testing
[3]https://leanpub.com/practical-web-test-automation
[4]https://leanpub.com/selenium-recipes-in-ruby
[5]https://leanpub.com/api-testing-recipes-in-ruby

- **Learn Ruby Programming by Examples**[6] by Zhimin Zhan and Courtney Zhan
  Master Ruby programming to empower you to write test scripts.

Tools

- **TestWise IDE**[7]
  AgileWay's next-generation functional testing IDE supports Selenium WebDriver and Appium.

- **BuildWise Server**[8]
  AgileWay's free and open-source continuous testing server, purposely designed for running automated UI tests with quick feedback.

- **BuildWise Agent**[9]
  AgileWay's BuildWise Agent that works with BuildWise server for parallel test execution.

---

[6]https://leanpub.com/learn-ruby-programming-by-examples-en
[7]http://testwisely.com/testwise
[8]http://testwisely.com/buildwise
[9]http://testwisely.com/buildwise

References

[Crispin & Gregory 09] Lisa Crispin and Janet Gregory. 2009. *Agile Testing*. Addison-Wesley Progressional.

[Shore & Warden 08] James Shore and Shane Warden. *The Art of Agile Development*. 2008. O'Reilly Media Inc.

[Kent Beck 04] Kent Beck. 2004. *Extreme Programming Explained: Embrace Change, 2nd Edition*, Addison-Wesley Progressional.

[Hunt & Thomas 00] Andrew Hunt and David Thomas. 2000. *The Pragmatic Programmer: From Journeyman to Master*. Addison-Wesley Progressional.

[Poppendieck 06] Mary Poppendieck. 2006. *Implementing Lean Software Development: From Concept to Cash*, Addison-Wesley Progressional.

[Whittaker 12] James Whittaker, Jason Arbon and Jeff Carollo. 2012. *How Google Tests Software*, Addison-Wesley.

[Fowler 00] Martin Fowler, "Continuous Integration (original version)" (posted Sep 10, 2010) http://martinfowler.com/articles/originalContinuousIntegration.html[10]

[Crispin 08] Lisa Crispin, "The Team's Pulse: CI/Build Process" (posted on Aug 23, 2010) http://lisacrispin.com/wordpress/2010/08/23/the-teams-pulse-cibuild-process[11]

[Copeland 10] uTest's interview "Testing the limits with Patrick Copeland" part 1 (Feburary 2010)
http://blog.utest.com/2010/02/22/testing-the-limits-with-patrick-copeland-part-i[12]

[Copeland 10-2] Patrick Copeland, uTest's interview "Testing the limits with Patrick Copeland" part 2 (Feburary 2010)
http://blog.utest.com/2010/02/22/testing-the-limits-with-patrick-copeland-part-i[13]

[Weinberg 18] Gerald Weinberg, "Testing is Harder than Development", TestGuild Podcast (September 09, 2018)
https://testguild.com/tribute-gerald-weinberg[14]

---

[10] http://martinfowler.com/articles/originalContinuousIntegration.html
[11] http://lisacrispin.com/wordpress/2010/08/23/the-teams-pulse-cibuild-process
[12] http://blog.utest.com/2010/02/22/testing-the-limits-with-patrick-copeland-part-i
[13] https://blog.utest.com/2010/02/23/testing-the-limits-with-patrick-copeland-part-ii/
[14] https://testguild.com/tribute-gerald-weinberg

[Page 15] Alan Page, "Testing Lessons Learned at Microsoft with Alan Page", TestGuild Podcast (March 17, 2015)
https://testguild.com/alan-page-principles-lessons-learned-at-microsoft/[15]

[Kent Beck 19], an interview with Kent Beck (September 15, 2019)
https://rackandstack-tech.blog/2019/10/15/kent-beck-fired-from-facebook/[16]

---

[15]https://testguild.com/alan-page-principles-lessons-learned-at-microsoft/
[16]https://rackandstack-tech.blog/2019/10/15/kent-beck-fired-from-facebook/

www.ingramcontent.com/pod-product-compliance
Lightning Source LLC
LaVergne TN
LVHW062310060326

832902LV00013B/2151